ROMANTIC

DAYS AND NIGHTS™ IN

ᏉANCOUVER

INTIMATE ESCAPES IN LOTUSLAND

by Barbara Braidwood and Richard Cropp

The
Globe
Pequot
Press

OLD SAYBROOK, CONNECTICUT

Cover photo: Michelle and Tom Grimm © International Stock Photo
Cover and text design: Lana Mullen
Illustrations: Maryann Dubé

Romantic Days and Nights is a trademark of The Globe Pequot Press.

Library of Congress Cataloging-in-Publication Data

Braidwood, Barbara.
    Romantic days and nights in Vancouver : intimate escapes in Lotusland / Barbara Braidwood and Richard Cropp. — 1st ed.
        p.   cm. — (Romantic cities series)
    Includes indexes.
    ISBN 0-7627-0203-6
    1. Vancouver (B.C.)—Guidebooks.   I. Cropp, Richard. II. Title. III. Series.
F1089.5.V22B73   1998
917.11'33—dc21   98-14830
                                         CIP

Manufactured in the United States of America
First Edition/First Printing

To my parents, Lois and Richard Braidwood, with love, affection and thanks
for all the encouragement you gave me to follow my dreams.
What a wonderful gift for my journey.
—Barbara

To Barbara's parents, Lois and Dick, my never ending gratitude
for the woman you created. Her humor, affection, and above all, her wisdom
have encouraged me to go to places I never would have gone alone.
It all flows through from you.
—Rick

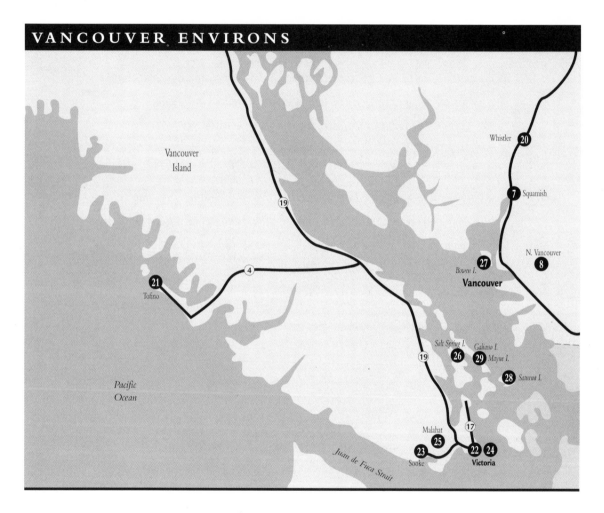

VANCOUVER ENVIRONS

Vancouver Island

Pacific
Ocean

Tofino **21**

4

19

Whistler **20**

7 Squamish

N. Vancouver
8

Bowen I. **27**
Vancouver

Salt Spring I. Galiano I.
19 **26** **29** Mayne I.

28 Saturna I.

Malahat
25

17

23 **22** **24**
Sooke **Victoria**

Juan de Fuca Strait

Numbers on map correspond to itinerary numbers (see Table of Contents).

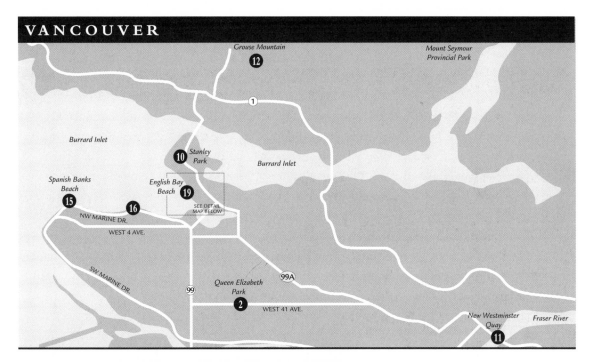

VANCOUVER

Grouse Mountain
12

Mount Seymour
Provincial Park

1

Burrard Inlet

Stanley
Park
10

English Bay
Beach
19

Burrard Inlet

Spanish Banks
Beach
15

16

NW MARINE DR.

WEST 4 AVE.

SEE DETAIL
MAP BELOW

SW MARINE DR.

Queen Elizabeth
Park

99A

99

2

WEST 41 AVE.

New Westminster
Quay

Fraser River

11

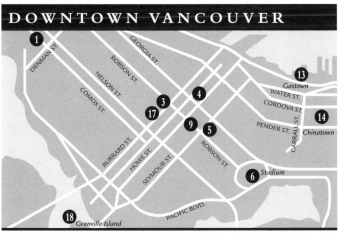

DOWNTOWN VANCOUVER

1

DENMAN ST.

GEORGIA ST.

ROBSON ST.

NELSON ST.

COMOX ST.

BURRARD ST.

HOWE ST.

SEYMOUR ST.

13

Gastown

WATER ST.

CORDOVA ST.

PENDER ST.

CARRALL ST.

14

Chinatown

4

3

17

9

5

ROBSON ST.

6

Stadium

18

Granville Island

PACIFIC BLVD.

ACKNOWLEDGMENTS

Everyone, it seems, loves romance. We received more help and suggestions from friends and strangers for this book than all the other books and articles we have ever written! And frankly, we were shocked at a few of the novel notions people have. Of course, it was important to be thorough for you, the reader, so in the name of research, we did try them all.

First we would like to thank the largest group of advisors--all those guys (all guys and one woman) who thought the parking lot at Jericho beach was the most romantic place in Vancouver. Uh, thanks, but that wasn't exactly what the women said. Just so you know next time.

Also, Mike Hagan, who probably could have written this book, sorry, we didn't include any of your thoughts here. I wasn't about to tell Barbara any of your ideas because she would wonder why I wasn't doing all those things for her.

We would also like to thank for their suggestions, rude and otherwise:

Jennifer Braidwood and Michael Beards
Dick Cropp
Jan Wilkinson
Janice Downing and George Eisler
Bridget Browning and Glen Browning
Ed DesRoches and Katie O'Brien
Alec Burke and Monica Smith
Susan M. Boyce
Barbara Shantz
Sandra Ecclestone and Tom Seifert
Nicole Ouellette
Lynda Cumming
John Bourassa
Poppy

Ben Hughes
Liam Culhane
Cecilia Ronderos and Alan Bridges
Pat and Al Telfer
Shirly Nilsson and Sly Chasteaneuf
Suzanne Schulhof and Mark Schulhof
Brendan Mann
Joy Clifton
Lisa McLean
Kaayla and Pat
Kitty and James
Michelle Wetteland
Michael Ladd

CONTENTS

The prices and rates listed in this guidebook are in Canadian dollars and were confirmed at press time. We recommend, however, that you call establishments before traveling to obtain current information.

*W*e met and fell in love in Vancouver, so you may take it with a gram of skepticism when we say this is the most romantic city in the world. Or come see for yourself.

Perched on the edge of the great Canadian wilderness, Vancouver's setting on the wild North Pacific in the heart of the Coast Mountains of British Columbia has scenery that nurtures romance. Nature engulfs you. Bears and cougars still come down to within sight of the busy downtown core. Where else can you ski in the morning on slopes that overlook the city, sail in the bay for the afternoon, and take in a world-class ballet in the evening? Where else can you meander through a superior art exhibit in the morning, smell the primeval rainforest spice on an afternoon walk, and savor the sunset with a beach picnic prepared by a renowned chef?

Super Natural British Columbia's southwest corner appeals to any romantic couple's sensuous side with a rich variety of exciting experiences, from the fun and boisterous to the serene. You don't have to sacrifice the sophisticated pleasures of a major metropolis to enjoy storm-swept beaches or snowy mountains.

Vancouver, Victoria, and the Gulf Islands—the Lotusland of North America—is a raucous blend of California laid-back and European tradition. Even the lay of the land is full of surprises. Vancouver, the city, lies hidden from the wrath of the North Pacific by Vancouver Island. Victoria, the capital of British Columbia, lies at the southern end of Vancouver Island. In between Vancouver and Victoria on Vancouver Island are the Gulf Islands, hotbed of counterculture and hideaway of the rich and famous. The islands each have a different feel and climate. Some are rainy and lush; others have attracted a large permanent getaway population with their sunny disposition. While we have selected some of the most romantic places for you to visit, don't be afraid to explore—there are dozens of other jewels to be enjoyed.

GETTING AROUND

Bicycles, ferries, buses, regular jet service, helicopters and float planes can get you anywhere in Lotusland. How you travel will often depend on how fast you want to arrive and how much you're willing to pay. Navigating around the cities of Vancouver and Victoria can be done by automobile or public transport, but in many cases walking is the best mode of transport. For the itineraries to the Gulf Islands, cars are not necessarily the best way to go. On some islands during summer, you'll want a bike to beat the traffic and enjoy the scenery once you disembark from the ferry. Also ask the places we suggest for overnight accommodations, whether they can put together packages that include air transportation.

CONTACT NUMBERS

BC Ferries: (250) 386–3431 in British Columbia or (888) 223–3779 outside British Columbia

Super Natural British Columbia: (604) 663–6000 or (800) 663–6000

Tourism Vancouver: (604) 683–2000

Tourism Victoria: (250) 953–2033

HELPFUL HINTS

Whales, eagles, and deer are plentiful, so bring your camera and binoculars.

Book ahead, especially if you're traveling during the peak periods of summer, Christmas, holiday weekends, and so on. If the places we suggest aren't available, reservation services at the tourism centers (see list of contact numbers) can help you find alternative accommodations. Don't go to the Gulf Islands in the summer without making reservations beforehand; you could end up sleeping in your car.

Don't plan your whole trip around a one-night stay. Some B&B establishments may have minimum-stay requirements on weekends, especially during the peak seasons. Check this out first so you can plan the rest of your trip accordingly.

When calling about lodging, always ask if special rates or packages are available. These may save you money or add little extras and are especially popular during the less busy seasons. Certainly ask about romance packages, as these are being added to hotel offerings all the time, but don't close off other opportunities. A spa or B&B package may work out to be a terrific deal.

If you can be flexible about your dates of travel, always say so. Your first choice may be more expensive if it's in high season, and by shifting a week, you could save yourself a hefty sum.

While hotel chains' toll-free numbers are a wonderful convenience, we suggest calling the hotels directly when dealing with larger establishments. More than once we've tried to track down a promotion through the toll-free number without success but then found it immediately when phoning the hotel directly.

Always inquire about an early check-in and late checkout if these best suit your schedule. Most places are more than willing to accommodate you if they can. We inquire first when we make our reservations, but if the answer is no, we check again on our day of arrival. Things change. Even if you can't check in early, inquire about leaving your bags while you explore.

Vancouver is a city of splendid views, and many restaurants are located to appreciate them. When making reservations, always ask whether a view is available from the restaurant and if so whether you can have a window seat. Though prime locations can rarely be guaranteed, most places will take note of your request and do what they can.

Most of these itineraries can be accomplished any day of the week. The majority of shops and attractions are open on Sundays in Vancouver, although the hours of operation may vary. Clearly, some events are available only on certain days. We have suggested brunch in a couple of places where it may not be available except on weekends; in such cases you would generally still be able to eat at the restaurant during the week but the brunch menu wouldn't be available. The price ranges mentioned are for an entree for the mealtime suggested. Prices are generally but not always different at lunch and dinner.

Several of these itineraries will fit together neatly for one- to two-week honeymoons or soul renewals. For example, you can ferry between the various islands without returning to the mainland each time. The people at BC Ferries (see Appendix) are helpful and can advise you about optimal scheduling. Be careful not to string too many outings together, for much of the charm of this part of the world lies in sitting in one spot and letting nature come to you.

Any of these itineraries would make a great pre- or postaddition to a leisurely cruise to Alaska. Why not? Three-quarters of the North American cruise ships use Vancouver for their home port during summer, and just about any day of the week you can watch luxury cruise ships depart from downtown Stanley Park or the beaches.

Wildlife and people don't mix. Do not under any circumstances approach bears or cougars. In spring, particularly when blueberries grow wild in the North Shore Mountains, bears forage along hiking trails.

The fact that you can see the city from the wilderness of the mountains lulls people's sense of caution. Each year many hikers are lost within sight of Vancouver, and on average one or two persons are never found. In 1996 a commercial passenger airliner that had disappeared in the 1950s was found in the mountains you can see from the city. Despite a concerted search, it took more than forty years to find the missing plane. Walk in the mountains; they are beautiful. But be aware of the weather, stay on well-marked walks and trails, and let someone know where you are.

Canada is metric. One kilometer is equal to $\frac{5}{8}$ mile. Prices are quoted in Canadian dollars. At the time of publication, a Canadian dollar was equal to about 70 U.S. cents. In other words, you get about $1.40 Canadian for each U.S. dollar. Canadian prices may seem a bit high unless you keep this 30 to 40 percent discount in mind.

DISCLAIMER

It's a fact of life that all guidebooks start going out of date the instant they're printed. The only thing not likely to change by more than a few centimeters is the distance between Vancouver and the islands. Prices, hours of operation, seasons, dates, availability, and even the names of hotels and restaurants can change at any time. Please be sure to confirm the details of your trip by phone before you start out. We can't take responsibility for the accuracy of information on road conditions, ferry schedules, and the like—we already know they'll change.

HELP US KEEP THIS GUIDE UP TO DATES

Every effort has been made by the authors and editors to make this guide as accurate and useful as possible. However, many things can change after a guide is published—establishments close, phone numbers change, facilities come under new management, etc.

We would love to hear from you concerning your experiences with this guide and how you feel it could be made better and be kept up to date. While we may not be able to respond to all comments and suggestions, we'll take them to heart and we'll make certain to share them with the authors. Please send your comments and suggestions to the following address:

The Globe Pequot Press
Reader Response/Editorial Department
P.O. Box 833
Old Saybrook, CT 06475

Or you may e-mail us at:

editorial@globe-pequot.com

Thanks for your input, and happy travels!

PULSE OF THE CITY

ITINERARY 1

Two days and one night

HEART OF THE WEST END

*L*ooking at all the high-rises it's hard to believe that less than fifty years ago this area was all low-rise apartments and single-family homes. The Sylvia Hotel on Beach Avenue just across the street from the beach was the tallest structure around. Now the area is the playground for thousands of people drawn by the excitement and romance of the city. Three blocks from the crowds, you can walk the serene paths of Stanley Park, admiring the rain-moist fall colors. A half-hour later you can be holding hands and sipping cappuccino on a heated outdoor patio. During summer, you can squander your days basking on the beach with all its entertaining vignettes and spend your evenings lost in each other on Second Beach, perhaps the most romantic beach in the city. It's all just part of the neighborhood of the West End.

Practical notes: The West End is compact. No place is more than a half-hour's stroll, so leave your car parked (parking available at the inn) and absorb the ambience.

DAY ONE: LATE MORNING/AFTERNOON

For a downtown oasis with easy access to English Bay Beach (2 blocks), Stanley Park (1 block), and the hustle and bustle of Denman Street (2 blocks), you can't ask for better than the **English Bay Inn** (1968 Comox Street; 604–683–8002; $160 to $275, with breakfast). The inn is a little jewel of a building slipped in among the dense high-rises of the city's West End. Built in the 1930s, the guest house has five beautiful rooms to chose from, each with private bath, beds smothered with rich linens, and antique decorations. Situated smack in the middle of a series of apartment complexes, the tranquil garden in the back will soothe and remove you from the surrounding city.

Romance at a Glance

♥ *Sip port at the English Bay Inn (604–683–8002).*

♥ *Enjoy brunch at the Riley Waterfront Café (604–684–3666).*

♥ *Tour False Creek by ferry.*

♥ *Engage in hands-on activities at Science World Museum (604–268–6363).*

♥ *Dine in style at the Teahouse Restaurant at Ferguson Point (604–669–3281).*

♥ *Nuzzle up on an Olde Tyme Carriage Ride (604–329–8611 or 604–439–9357).*

For an extra touch of romance, go for Room 5. It's a two-room suite on two levels at the top of the house, with a view of the garden from the sitting room. The sitting room is cozily decorated with an overstuffed print sofa and chair, and your own decanter of port sits on the side table for an intimate drink for two at your whim. A pocket door hides the stairway to the loft bedroom. Up there, at the top of the house, is another sofa placed in front of the fireplace, a pillow-covered sleigh bed, and a bathroom with a 6-foot whirlpool tub. The owner, Bob Chapin, has recently renovated a house across the street as well, where he also has a couple of beautiful antique-furnished rooms.

If you arrive in the morning, you'll be a tad early to check in, so leave both your car (parking is free at the inn) and your bags at the English Bay Inn and take a cab over to the Riley Waterfront Café for brunch. Leaving your car behind will allow you a beautiful walk back to the inn along the beachfront seawall and lively Denman Street (about a half-hour's walk).

Brunch

We love the **Riley Waterfront Café** (1661 Granville Street; 604–684–3666, $8 to $12) for weekend brunch. A variety of egg dishes—omelets, Benedict, or scrambles—come with plump, seasoned home fries and some of the best multigrain bread in the city, and the glass front and over-water deck mean you can't beat the view. If breakfast food is not to your liking, you'll find plenty of other selections. You won't go away hungry—the servings are immense.

The waterfront cafe looks over to Granville Island and is tucked under the Granville Street Bridge, which spans False Creek. In good weather sit outside, where you can hear the activity on the harbor. As you eat, indoors or out, you'll be in an excellent position to observe the show as private pleasurecraft depart for a day of water fun from the marinas in False Creek. Watching canoes, skiffs, sailboats, barges, fishing trawlers, tugs, dance boats, and waterfowl negotiate the narrow waterway is as exciting as a stock-car race. Especially when there is a waterborne parade or a regatta, the inlet looks more like an overdrawn cartoon than real life, as boats jockey, collide, sink, swamp, and sputter. Some even make it to sea.

You can't miss the multicolored ferries carrying people around the creek. This unique transport system covers the waterfront of False Creek from the Planetarium near Kits Beach to Science World at the end of the inlet. To access the ferries, go out the front door of the cafe and turn left toward the Burrard Street Bridge. **Aquabus**'s (604–689–5858; point-to-point rates start at $1.75, depending on the route) twelve-passenger boats dock at the foot of Hornby Street—about 2 blocks away. Just walk along the waterfront and you'll see the dock and the sign, or watch where the ferries land.

For a $4.00 fee you are ferried from Hornby Street to the dropoff point for **Science World** (1455 Quebec Street; 604–268–6363; open Monday to Friday 10:00 A.M. to 5:00 P.M. and Saturday, Sunday, and holidays 10:00 A.M. to 6:00 P.M.; allow two to three hours; $10.50 for entrance to Science World or $13.50 to include the **Alcan Omnimax Theatre**) in fifteen to eighteen minutes. You'll travel along the length of False Creek, passing by the houseboats in the floating village, as well as a couple of marinas, and getting a waterside view of the downtown skyline. Take along your camera, as you're likely to see great blue herons and loons as you pass. And with luck you might see the sweating precision of the world-renowned dragon-boat racers as they practice for regattas (Vancouver's team won first place in Hong Kong a few years ago).

A visit to this hands-on museum and activity center housed in a geodesic dome is a must for lovers. Don't miss the parabolic Whisper Dishes, where your murmured sweet nothings are directed across the interior of the hall to your loved one on the far side with no wires or radios, just whisper power. At the Shadow Wall place your bodies far apart except for your lips—hold that pose and watch your shadows stay on the screen as you move away. We found the Shadow Wall to be the most fun when we used exaggerated gestures; try it out.

Depending on the showing schedule, try to see a film at the Alcan OMNIMAX Theatre. It's one of the largest dome screens in the world, with a 27-meter diameter, 5-story-high screen and a 28-speaker-digital sound system. The films change every six months, and usually there are two films to choose from. Sit as high in the audience as you can so that the picture totally fills your vision. Any film with flight in it is guaranteed to give you a physical thrill, as the all-encompassing view of the screen fools your body into thinking you're flying.

On the way back take the ferry ($4.00) to **Granville Island** (Granville Island; 604–666–6655). You'll be dropped off almost directly across the water from the Riley Waterfront Café next to the waterfront entrance to **Granville Island Public Market.** Stop and listen to the musicians or watch a magic show in the market courtyard before drifting inside. Browse around even if you don't want to shop. You'll generally find merchants with leather goods, jewelry, and pottery alongside the fresh fruits and vegetables, pâtés, cheeses, seafoods, meats, baked goods, fudge tables, food counters, and flower stalls.

If you get the urge to nibble, you're in the right place. Expect it to happen. Your senses will be assaulted with a bouquet of aromas—from sweet spices to fresh-baked bread—that will be hard to resist. We highly recommend the freshly baked doughnuts, hot from the oven and buttery-sweet (near the center front entrance). Grab a cup of coffee or espresso to go from one of the many coffee shops and head out to listen to the street performers. Performers at the market are generally good-quality local groups, and some are downright terrific. Expect anything from Japanese drums to jazz to country-and-western.

Or go out one of the front doors of the market and make your way to **La Baguette and L'Echarlotte** in Triangle Square. Set in the middle of the square, almost in the parking lot and in front of a big yellow building just to your right, the bakery features terrific goodies and is another great spot for street entertainment.

Wander around. Right behind you (from Triangle Square) is the **Net Loft,** with a variety of twenty-four craft stores and art studios. The shops will entice you to splurge on everything from hats, glasses, and jewelry to handmade paper goods. Some of the stores feature the unique works of local artists, while others import exotic wares. Inside is yet another cafe and musicians' venue. Especially on rainy days, this is the place to be. The island is also home to numerous studios and galleries whose creations range from ceramics to silks and from sculptures and pottery to metals and glass. Most of the artists are delighted for you to come in to watch them work.

When you are weary, take the ferry across False Creek and walk back to the inn for quiet time and a glass of port or sherry before dinner.

DAY ONE: EVENING
Dinner

Don't despair if it's a rainy or cloudy sunset when you go to **The Teahouse Restaurant** at Ferguson Point (7501 Stanley Park Drive; 604–669–3281; entrees range from $17 to $25). This old military base on a bluff at the edge of the sea in the midst of the Stanley Park Forest offers one of the most spectacular views of the sunset in Vancouver. But with the addition many years ago of the large, all-glass conservatory, even dining in the rain is a charming

Eventually everyone who visits Vancouver arrives at the Teahouse. Past guests include former Canadian prime ministers Pierre Trudeau and Brian Mulroney, as well as the prime ministers of Germany and Australia and the president of Chile. More important, the past and present captains of the Starship Enterprise *and the whole Toronto Maple Leafs hockey team have chosen to refuel here. All movie stars make their way to the restaurant, and some of the most famous among them include Michael Douglas, Kirstie Alley, Richard Gere, and Tom Selleck.*

experience, akin to picnicking in a spring shower without getting wet. Indoor rubber plants and dramatic outdoor lighting filtering up through the giant trees add to the dinner-in-the-forest effect. Candlelight graces the linen-covered tables with subtle shadows. Seating in the conservatory is the most popular, and any seat in the house has a view of the sunset; for a little privacy, though, try the table for two in the fenced-off area of the drawing room.

We do recommend you share the Teahouse Mushrooms, packed with a thick, cheesy combination of crab and scallions, for an appetizer. Follow this signature dish with the rich and creamy carrot soup—some of the best we've ever had—before moving on to the entrees, which are all finely presented and scrumptious. Lamb lovers should definitely order a rack of woolly here; it's tender and succulent. But save room for dessert, maybe the Delight of the King, a pastry swan filled with rum custard and whipped cream, with a dark chocolate sauce, that's a visual treat and, once you succumb to temptation and put your fork into it, delectable.

After dinner forget the car and take a ride by horse and carriage with **Olde Tyme Carriage Rides** (604–329–8611 or 604–439–9357; special bookings priced from \$75 for a half-hour). Snuggle together in the Cinderella carriage and ride through the evening around the park. The ride seems to touch people's romantic souls, and many a marriage proposal has been tendered as the horse clops around town.

DAY TWO: MORNING
Breakfast

Breakfast is in the Gothic-style dining room on the second floor of the inn. The elegant room, with Persian carpet, peach-colored walls, roaring fire (weather-dependent), fresh flowers, and ornately carved high-backed chairs in rich wood, will greet you as you enter. Everyone eats together at the one long dining table, and owner Bob Chapin is there to get the conversational ball rolling if the crowd is shy. You'll feast on fresh scones and a fruit plate laden with ten to twelve different fruits, such as mangoes, grapes, and kiwis. The main dish could be omelets with shrimp and crab, or poached eggs with lox, or phyllo pastry with peppers, chicken, mushrooms, Camembert cheese, chutney, and garlic. Mmmm.

After breakfast stroll around Lost Lagoon, the lake on the West End side of Stanley Park, which is a short 2 blocks from the inn. Not only are the trails along the lagoon especially pleasant, with colorful landscaping and quaint stone and wooden bridges crossing small streams, but wildlife is tame everywhere. Whole families of skunks and raccoons, sometimes as many as twenty or thirty, make a good living from tourists (so much so that some of these critters have been heard to growl and turn up their noses when offerings are not from the better bakeries and eateries along Denman Street!). Swans and a variety of ducks have staked out the waterfront for families (nice to watch, but don't approach), and most of the year you can see Canada geese too lazy and fat to fly south. All the inhabitants are in the family way by late spring, and the whole area is a wonderful crazy quilt of clumsy chicks and miniature balls of fur.

FOR MORE ROMANCE

The two of you can walk along Lost Lagoon after dark. In the center of the lagoon is a fountain spouting columns of water reflecting multicolored lights at its base. The pattern changes constantly, except in midwinter, when the whole fountain freezes into a crystalline white abstract sculpture.

ITINERARY 2
One day

WRITTEN IN THE STARS

From the top of Little Mountain after dark, the North Shore Mountains are painted slightly darker than the night sky. The city lights of West and North Vancouver create luminous waves on the mountain's mural, and downtown skyscrapers needle the canvas from below. With a gentle spring rain, a floating white mantle of snow or the fiery tempest of fall, you're still warm and dry next to the fireplace or within the glass bubble of the arboretum.

Practical notes: Little Mountain (Queen Elizabeth Park) is one of our favorite parks at any time of the year. You can wander the gardens and see the arboretum year-round, and in good weather you can play par-three golf on the hilltop course.

AFTERNOON
Lunch

Start your afternoon with a bit of spice at one of the best Thai restaurants in the city. The surroundings at the **Chao Phraya Thai Restaurant** (1505 West 2nd Avenue, at the entrance to Granville Island; 604–732–3939; $8 to $15) are bright and cheery with a view of the marina, Granville Island, and the seawall; the service is friendly; and the food is authentic Thai (not California or French Fusion Thai, but real Thai). The large selection of traditional dishes, served family style, are all made with fresh ingredients, many shipped from Thailand each week. (No prefab food here, the bean sprouts snap and crunch in your mouth.) The restaurant is very popular and has a regular clientele who congregate from all over the city. We recommend the vegetarian curry (the coconut sauce is delectable) and the Pad Thai: stir fried Thai-style vermicelli noodles with sprouts and ground peanuts. The only accommodation the restaurant has made to the western palate is that you can ask to have the food mildly spicy rather than life threatening. Wash it all down with Singha beer, Thailand's premier pale larger, and finish off by splitting a mango and sticky black rice dessert. The mango is fresh from Thailand and lushly sweet.

ɕ╳ɔ

After lunch carry on along Cambie Street to Thirty-third Street. It's possible to spend hours in the dome of the **Bloedel Floral Conservatory** (Queen Elizabeth Park, Cambie at Thirty-third; 604–257–8570; 10:00 A.M. to 5:00 P.M. in winter and to 8:00 P.M. in summer; $3.25; wheelchair accessible), especially on a rainy, blustery winter day. No matter what the temperature outside, inside it's balmy. The conservatory houses an amazing collection of 500 species and varieties of plants from warmer climes. Dozens of tropical birds fly freely among the jungle and desert terrains. You need only to stand quietly with your eyes closed and your senses open for a taste of warm vacations yet to come.

Outside the glass dome, crowning the peak of the hill in the park, is a quarry that has been reworked into a masterpiece of gardening. The lush grounds are filled with formal gardens, streams, and waterfalls, all complemented with a view of the city skyline. You'll find paths to wander, bridges to cross, and quiet

Romance at a Glance
- ♥ *Munch superb food at the Chao Phraya Thai Restaurant (604–875–6999).*
- ♥ *Visit the arboretum at the Bloedel Floral Conservatory (604–257–8570).*
- ♥ *Play par-three golf and admire the view (604–874–8336).*
- ♥ *Dine in front of the fireplace at Seasons in the Park (604–874–8008).*
- ♥ *Take a late-night peek at Venus's curves (604–738–2855).*

benches to rest on. The area has long been a favorite spot for wedding photos, and on a sunny day you might see as many as a dozen couples with their entourages.

We got our par-three golfing start on the course at **Queen Elizabeth Park Pitch and Putt** (Queen Elizabeth Park; 604–874–8336, open February to November, 7:30 A.M. to dusk; $7.40 summer rates but discounted to $4.35 one hour before twilight) and fell in love with the undulating contours of the course bathed in soft evening light. Weeping willows surround the fairways, and the greens follow the gentle sweep of the hill as the course meanders up and over it. Peekaboo views out over the city and surrounding neighborhoods emphasize the park's serenity, and laughter carries a long way in the quiet. Par three is played on a course a third the size of a real golf course. You can rent everything you need at the clubhouse. Or skip whacking the ball and just meander the course beneath the willows, arm in arm—it's that kind of romantic place.

EVENING
Dinner

There are no bad seats in the enchanting, glass-enclosed **Seasons in the Park** (at the top of Queen Elizabeth park between Cambie and Thirty-third; 604–874–8008; $14 to $24). Set in three tiers, the tables all have a sweeping view out over the park of the Vancouver skyline and the North Shore Mountains. Our favorite seat on cold winter nights is in the main dining room, on the upper tier next to the fireplace. We recommend the eggplant and tomato terrine for starters, and for an entree have the baked herb-crusted Chilean sea bass or the grilled herbed loin of veal. The service is attentive without being cloying.

◈◈◈

Comets have been known to make women swoon and men stutter in fear, so if unnerving your partner is part of your seduction routine, check out what's happening at the **Gordon MacMillan Southam Observatory** (the small dome in Vanier Park next to the

It was a country affair and the ultimate romance that touched everyone's life. Bill Clinton and Boris Yeltsin dined at Seasons in the Park during the Vancouver Summit, April 3, 1993.

Planetarium at 1100 Chestnut Street; usually open Friday and Saturday and during celestial events; phone the Skyline for details, 604–738–2855; free admission). Although not the most powerful lens in Canada, the 0.5-meter telescope is easily accessible to the public late into the night many times a year. Especially when something fascinating has developed in the heavens—which is, according to stargazers, most nights—the telescope is staffed by volunteers who can guide you around the moons of Jupiter or the curves of Venus. Dress warmly, as the observatory is not heated and frequently the best viewing is late at night when it's cooler. If you've never peeked through a large telescope, this is an experience not to be missed. Besides, it gives you an opportunity to share a little warmth.

FOR MORE ROMANCE

The **Pacific Space Center,** also known as the H. R. MacMillan Planetarium (1100 Chestnut Street on Kits Point; 604–738–7827; open 10:00 to 5:00 P.M. Tuesday to Sunday, until 8:00 P.M. Friday, and closed Monday; $12), is adjacent to the telescope and has exhibits and shows guaranteed to get you starry-eyed. Sitting way back in the recliners and watching the stars are an easy way to spend a rainy afternoon. Rock laser shows also play on some weekends and start at 9:30 P.M., so if you want to while away some time before a celestial event at the telescope, see what's on.

ITINERARY 3
One day

CHOCOLATE ECSTASY

*C*hocolate. Sinfully rich, creamy, and silky-soft to the tongue. A food we use to treat ourselves or to express ourselves to others. Milk, semisweet, bitter, or dark chocolate. Solid or liquid. Pure or mixed with other sugary-sweet ingredients. Given sometimes as a form of apology but more often as a gesture of love and affection. And too rarely an indulgence that we simply give to ourselves.

Indulgence. What this day is all about.

Practical notes: Anticipation is a wonderful thing. And so, in anticipation of this outing, we have a suggestion: Cutting down on your dessert consumption for a week or two beforehand wouldn't be amiss with this itinerary. And don't plan anything too hectic for the next day—between the sugar rush and the chocolate, you could be up very late the night you choose to do this itinerary.

MORNING
Breakfast

Start off your morning with coffee and a snack at the **Kits Coffee Company** (2198 West Fourth Avenue; 604–739–0139; open 7:00 A.M. to 11:00 P.M. Friday and Saturday and closing at

9:00 P.M. the remainder of the week). You can get a choice of muffins, buns, cakes, and pastries, along with a wide range of coffees.

❧

For a classic kind of chocolate shop, stop in at **Purdy's Chocolates** (2196 West Fourth Avenue; 604–730–8669) next door. **Chocolate Arts** (2037 West Fourth Avenue; 604–739–0475), down the street, is aptly named. It's not just a candy store; some of the works are so delicate that it's hard to sink your teeth into them and thereby destroy the art. Chocolate Arts was started in 1989 by Greg Hook, who trained as a pastry chef. His partner, Robert Davidson, is an aboriginal artist.

The box of six Chocolate Medallions with a Pacific Coast Indian motif ($14) is a wonder. The medallions have three designs originally carved by Davidson: Haida Frog, Haida Moon, and Killer Whale. All were originally carved in wood and some were cast in silver and gold for pendants and jewelry. The chocolate molds are first hand-painted with Belgian bittersweet chocolate to accurately reflect the design. The filling is a mixture of chopped hazelnuts and dried organic blueberries. Or you can purchase single medallions for $2.25 each.

For a single chocolate to pop in your mouth, try a Cleopatra, in a pyramid-shaped, milk- and dark-chocolate, caramel-cream-filled truffle. Or opt for a Romeo, filled with blackberry cream and blackberry ganache (sorry, no Juliets).

Back in your car, drive over to the shopping mecca, Robson Street, to continue your search for chocolate delights. The **Rocky Mountain Chocolate Factory** (1017 Robson Street; 604–688–4100; open 10:00 A.M. to 9:00 P.M. daily) will tempt you with not only an array of chocolates but also a wide

Romance at a Glance

♥ *Stoke your engines with breakfast at the Kits Coffee Company (604–739–0139).*

♥ *Check out chocolate creations at Chocolate Arts (604–739–0475).*

♥ *Test other candy shops.*

♥ *Cater to body and soul at the Robert Andrew Salon and Spa (604–687–7133).*

♥ *Indulge your chocolate fantasies at the Fleuri Restaurant (604–682–5511).*

Flowers are another way to express love and affection for a cherished one. When you're at Chocolate Arts, buy a tulip ($14)—solid milk chocolate with a dark-chocolate stem—and present it to your loved one. A flower and chocolate combined—how much better can life be? Well, you could add a chocolate wine bottle for $20.

variety of fudges made right on the premises. Look for the popular Oreo Fudge or the pink-colored Burgundy Cherry Fudge. At Halloween you might see Pumpkin Fudge; Christmas, Egg Nog Fudge. The staff may be whipping up a batch in the big copper bowl (situated for prime viewing in the window facing the street) when you drop by. When they're not making fudge, they create prodigious vats of caramel apples, brittles, and Rocky Pop (caramel popcorn). And if you still haven't had enough, wander along to **Daniel, Le Chocolat Belge** (1105 Robson Street; 604–688–9624; open 10:00 A.M. to 9:00 P.M. Thursday and Friday, 12:00 to 6:00 P.M. Sunday, and 10:00 A.M. to 6:00 P.M. the remainder of the week) and see if the staff can tempt you with their selection of chocolates. All are sold by the gram.

AFTERNOON
Lunch

A wide selection of eateries can also be found along Robson Street. Try the **Settebello Restaurant** (1133 Robson Street on the second floor; 604–681–7377; lunch and dinner, 11:30 A.M. to 10:00 P.M.; prices range from $13 for a pizza to about $18 for entrees) for a different pizza. Although there are various pastas and heartier fare, we recommend that the two of you try one of the tasty pizzas with your choice of sun-dried tomatoes, capers, oyster mushrooms, and an assortment of spicy meats.

ॐ

After lunch, make your way to the **Robert Andrew Salon and Spa** (lower level, Hotel Vancouver, 900 West Georgia; 604–687–7133; open daily) for some pampering. The appealing clean lines of the salon's interior design won an award at the 1997 Ninth Annual Canadian Stylist of the Year Awards Ceremony and the staff is friendly and efficient.

Spoil yourselves with a full range of services, from hairstyling, facials (which include a neck-and-shoulder massage), and hand and foot care to aromatherapy hydropack wraps. Packages combining an array of services to cater to your every need last from two to six hours. And men are not left out: A combination package is set up for men only.

Whichever you choose, don't leave without a massage. Peering over counters in candy stores can give you a crick in your neck. After an hour under the magic fingers of the staff at Robert Andrew Salon and Spa, you'll feel supple and ready to carry on into the evening.

EVENING

Dessert

Tonight's food and entertainment is chocolate. The "all-you-can-eat" Chocoholic Bar takes place at the **Fleuri Restaurant** (The Sutton Place Hotel, 845 Burrard Street; 604–682–5511; $13.95 alone or $5.75 with dinner; available Thursday through Saturday evenings). Dinner? We never eat much before the Chocoholic Bar, but if you need something in your stomach to soak up the chocolate, you can get a full meal right at the Fleuri Restaurant.

What does one find at a Chocoholic Bar? A host of temptations guaranteed to keep you returning to the table again and again. Black Forest Fudge, Mint Chocolate Truffle Cake, White Chocolate Charlotte, Chocolate Bourbon Mousse, Chocolate Cheesecake, Chocolate

Hay Stacks, Chocolate Bread Pudding, Chocolate Fruit Pizza . . . more than enough choices to keep a chocolate lover happy. Also here is a varied selection of ice creams (including vanilla for the purists in the crowd) and light and refreshing sorbets to help keep your tongue from becoming numb to the chocolate.

At some point squeeze in the Chocoholic Bar specialty dessert: Hot Brittany Crepes, oozing with ice cream and dripping with toppings. The crepes are made fresh by the pastry chef at the buffet table as you watch. Try this dessert the way the staff likes it, with the crepe folded around the ice cream to hasten the melting, and then pile on the nuts, melted chocolate, sprinkles, chocolate chips, ganache, icing sugar, liqueurs—virtually anything your hearts desire.

Can't even think of sleep? Stroll over to **Club Millennium** (fifth floor, 595 Hornby Street; 604–684–2000; cover charge of $5 to $10, depending on the day of the week; open 8:00 P.M. to 2:00 A.M. daily, except Monday, when it's closed) and get rid of some of that excess energy.

This upscale club features live music on Thursday, Friday, and Saturday nights that ranges from Motown to rock to big band. Special guest appearances and a Las Vegas–style revue performed by the staff make this a little different from most other clubs in Vancouver. The club boasts a sizable dance floor, velvet-covered booths, a super ventilation system with the cigar-smoking crowd in mind, and a more intimate area away from the music and crowds, where it's possible to have a quiet conversation.

FOR MORE ROMANCE

Indulge in an overnight stay at the **Hotel Vancouver** (900 West Georgia Street; 604–684–3131 or 800–441–1414). Inquire about packages that include one- or two-night accommodations, breakfast, free access to the health club, and a Robert Andrew Salon and Spa gift certificate. Rooms start at $195.

ITINERARY 4
One day and one night

ALL THAT JAZZ

*J*azz was popular thirty to thirty-five years ago in Vancouver but was eclipsed by disco in the 1970s. Diehard jazz musicians hung in to watch a resurgence of local jazz in a dozen permutations and fusion with salsa, Brazilian, African, and acid-rock sounds. Now musicians from all over the continent include Vancouver on the circuit, and local bands have developed their own following.

Today's itinerary is the perfect excuse for the two of you to slip into a languorous mid-afternoon nap. You'll need your strength for tonight.

Practical notes: The **Jazz Hotline** (604–682–0706), updated by the Coastal Jazz and Blues Society, is your twenty-four hour lifeline to what's happening in the city each week. Also track down a copy of the *Georgia Straight* newspaper, a free arts-and-entertainment rag available everywhere. The concierge at your hotel may have a copy, or step out the front door, turn right and proceed 2 blocks to the Book Warehouse bookstore for a free copy. As you would expect, most performances are on Thursday, Friday, and Saturday evenings and Sunday afternoons.

DAY ONE: AFTERNOON

Check in at the four-diamond **Listel Vancouver** (1300 Robson Street; 604–684–8461; $120 to $270), in the heart of the upscale shopping district of Robson Street. The hotel boasts a unique concept, with guest rooms styled as individual art galleries featuring original paintings, sculpture, and limited editions. Each of the rooms on the two Gallery Floors is devoted to a different artist whose work is tastefully displayed. In partnership with the **Buschlen Mowatt Galleries** and the **Keith Alexander Gallery,** the hotel has filled sixty of its rooms with works from artists such as Yehouda Chaki, Helen Frankenthaler, Z. Z. Wei, and the French national treasure Jean Pierre Cassigneul.

If you're interested in purchasing any of the artwork in your room, speak with the hotel management or the people in the galleries. Just a few blocks from the hotel is the Buschlen Mowatt Galleries (1445 West Georgia Street; 604–682–1234; open 10:00 A.M. to 6:00 P.M. Monday to Saturday and 12:00 to 5:00 P.M. Sunday). Wander in just to see what else the gallery has to offer; it brings world-class exhibits to the city and is well worth the visit. The Keith Alexander Gallery (647 Howe Street; 604–682–7777) focuses on regional art and is located 1 block north of the Vancouver Art Gallery.

Romance at a Glance

♥ *Slumber in an art gallery at Listel Vancouver (604–684–8461).*

♥ *Snack and jam at Rossini's Pasta Palazzo (604–737–8080).*

♥ *Dine with the upbeat jazz at O'Doul's Restaurant and Bar (604–661–1400).*

♥ *Do the jazz circuit in town (604–682–0706).*

♥ *End in the early morning at the Georgia Street Bar and Grill (604–602–0994).*

Late Lunch

After checking in at the hotel, zip over to **Rossini's Pasta Palazzo** near Kit's Beach (1525 Yew Street; 604–737–8080; $10 minimum food and beverage charge during jamming) for an afternoon of jazz. The fun starts at 3:00 P.M., when the band of the week has friends and other musicians drop by for a bit of jamming. It's always entertaining, and reservations are recommended.

DAY ONE: EVENING
Dinner

You'd expect Creole and jambalaya at a restaurant featuring live jazz, and the Creole Tiger Prawns and Pacific Northwest Jambalaya are terrific—but there's something better. We got the message when we looked at all the other diners surrounding us and noticed that every hand held a steak knife. Having tried several items from the menu, we can unequivocally recommend **O'Doul's Restaurant and Bar** (1300 Robson Street; 604–661–1400; live jazz weekends, Thursday to Saturday; entrees $18 to $23) for a sizzling and tender steak and the most succulent lamb in the city. The grainy Dijon-crusted rack of lamb with rosemary jus candied shallots tops the list of taste treats (we'd even settle for the mashed potatoes with the rosemary jus). There's no point going to O'Doul's and missing the smoked chicken artichoke Brie strudel with champagne butter as an appetizer, which is as decadent as it sounds, or the smooth Belgian-chocolate terrine or vanilla bean crème brûlée for dessert. All are so rich, they should be shared.

Choose a table at the back of the restaurant, away from the piano, for quieter conversation; you'll still be able to easily hear the music. The outside walls are almost completely windows, so seats are great for watching the passing crowds on busy Robson Street. Or face the interior to absorb the ambience. Look up to the atrium ceiling, dominated by an antique twin-hemisphere map in shades of rose. The intimate feel of the restaurant is enhanced by the many skylights, indirect lighting, and rich glossy woodwork. Call O'Doul's Restaurant and Bar for a monthly schedule of who's playing.

After dinner you can visit several places of note (musical, of course). One of the oldest jazz clubs in town, the **Hot Jazz Society** (2120 Main Street; 604–873–4131), still has traditional

Jazzy Cupid

So you can hardly carry a tune but you just know that the joy of your life would love to be serenaded—you know, those smoky tunes of yesteryear, the embodiment of mystery, love, and romance. Find out where Sibel Thrasher is singing (see Practical Notes), go a half-hour early, and ask for the best seats in the house. (We suggest avoiding the front row; more than once the sound has been overpowering. Midroom or even at the back is preferable.) Sibel is a fixture of the jazz/blues scene in Vancouver and loves a good time. Her Billy Holiday/Ella Fitzgerald sound (no glasses shattered yet, but close) and showmanship have kept us up well past bedtime and completely hoarse on more than one occasion. Many of the venues she plays have a small dance floor so put on your dancing shoes. She'll get your message across for you.

Dixieland, New Orleans, and big-band music. The **Cotton Club** on Granville Island (200–1833 Anderson Avenue; 604–738–7465, music every night; $3.00 cover Thursday through Saturday and occasionally more for special guest appearances) also uses its baby grand for more traditional and New Orleans–style music (Doc Fingers would feel right at home here). You can find just about anything at the **Latin Quarter Restaurant** (1305 Commercial Drive; 604–251–1144), a small venue with only six or seven seats at the bar and a few tables; entrees range from $9 to $16.

At the **Georgia Street Bar and Grill** (801 West Georgia Street; 604–602–0994), it's appropriate to wear your evening gown and fur or break out your dinner jacket, but more casual clothes are certainly not a problem. You never know what kind of crowd you'll find, but the music is always good. The bar has been around for several years and has grown in popularity among jazz fans, so arrive at least an hour before the entertainment starts (call to check, but it's usually 9:30 P.M. or so) for a good seat.

FOR MORE ROMANCE

Rossini's Pasta Palazzo (604–737–8080) has been the home for many years of Linton Garner, who at eighty-three is still charming audiences with traditional jazz pieces five nights a week. You can catch him Tuesday to Saturday after 8:00 P.M.

Visit the city in June and you'll be able to partake of the ten-day International Jazz Festival. Free and ticketed performances take place at both indoor and outdoor venues around the city. Call the Jazz Hotline (604–682–0706) for details.

PLAYING AROUND

*B*ig and small, glittery and casual—the Vancouver theater scene has it all, from the glitz and glamour of the Ford Centre for the Performing Arts to the cozier atmosphere of the Main Stage or the Review Theatre at the Arts Club Theatre on Granville Island. If you love live theater, the two of you can spend the entire weekend as far away as the playwright's imagination can take you.

Practical notes: For information on the arts in Vancouver, call the **Arts Hotline** (604–684–ARTS [684–2787]), a twenty-four-hour recorded listing of arts events. You can choose from a number of selections, including theater and dance. For personal assistance call between 9:00 A.M. and 5:00 P.M. Monday to Friday.

The Orpheum, the Queen Elizabeth Theatre, and the Vancouver Playhouse are owned by the City of Vancouver and operated by Vancouver Civic Theatres. You can find out what's on at each venue by calling the Talking Yellow Pages (604–299–9000). Dial local 8050 for the Orpheum, local 8051 for the Queen Elizabeth Theatre, and local 8052 for the Vancouver Playhouse.

DAY ONE: AFTERNOON

Location, location, location. With the recently renovated **Metropolitan Hotel** (645 Howe Street; 604–687–1122 or 800–667–2300; from $269), you are certainly getting that. It's right in the center of the hustle and bustle. Despite its 18 stories and 197 rooms, it manages to preserve an elegant and intimate feeling. Known for its personalized service, the hotel is a member of Preferred Hotels and Resorts Worldwide.

When you call to reserve a room, inquire about any theater packages (valid from October through April) that might be available. Past packages have included deluxe accommodations, a three-course dinner at Diva at the Met, and parking. Alternatively, the Romance Package gives you a Junior Suite (a combination bedroom–living room with an oversize bathroom that has a soaker tub and a separate shower) with a bottle of sparkling wine and strawberries when you arrive and breakfast by room service or downstairs at Diva at the Met.

At this hotel the pool is a delightful place to spend time. It's not tucked away in a basement: it's on the third floor, and one wall and part of the ceiling are glass. The Jacuzzi tub is perched beside it so you can enjoy the light of the day. Even some of the exercise bikes are situated in front of the window. Afterward recline out on the deck and order a refreshing drink from room service before heading back to your room.

Romance at a Glance

♥ *Rest easy at the Metropolitan Hotel (604–687–1122 or 800–667–2300).*

♥ *Snack on a deli lunch at Rosie's on Robson (604–689–4499).*

♥ *Wander the streets of the Entertainment District.*

♥ *Savor the flavors at Diva at the Met (604–602–7788).*

♥ *Munch brunch at Remington's Restaurant (604–873–1811).*

Lunch

Stop in at **Rosie's on Robson** (298 Robson Street; 604–689–4499; $5 to $19; open 6:30 A.M. to approximately midnight)

Legend has it that when entering or exiting the Metropolitan Hotel, one must rub the head of the Foo Dogs that grace the doorway out front for good luck. A romantic weekend away means you are lucky in love, so why not give the Foo Dogs a rub and see what other good things can happen to you? You'll see by the smooth section on the center of the dogs' foreheads that many people believe this good-luck story—or at least are unwilling to take the chance that it's not true!

for a bite to eat. It's conveniently located just behind the library and, with its many show posters adorning the walls, will put you in the mood for entertainment. If you think you've missed what's happening in the city, look inside the front cover of the menu and read the rundown of what's going on in Vancouver. A deli-style restaurant and bar, Rosie's features a wide range of sandwiches, burgers, and other deli foods to choose from. We love the marinated artichoke and feta salad with mixed greens and a five-herb vinaigrette and, for a little comfort food, share the Babba's rice pudding, made with cream, honey, and raisins.

❧

This afternoon take a stroll through the area that has recently become known as the Entertainment District of Vancouver. In close proximity to one another are the Queen Elizabeth Theatre Complex (comprised of the Queen Elizabeth Theatre and the Vancouver Playhouse), General Motors Place and BC Place Stadium, the Vancouver Public Library, and the Ford Centre for the Performing Arts with the Orpheum not far away. Now is a good time to pick up tickets at the ticket office; you can relax longer over dinner if you don't have to add waiting time in the lineup.

From Rosie's take a left to Smithe Street and then turn right. At Seymour Street you'll see the **Orpheum** (Smithe Street at Seymour Street; 604–665–3050; for tickets call

604–280–4444), which seats 2,788. It was built in 1927 and is the home of the Vancouver Symphony Orchestra, the Vancouver Bach Choir, the Vancouver Cantata Singers, and the Vancouver Chamber Choir. The acoustics at this National Heritage Site make it a favorite for musical performances—everything from classical, rock, jazz, pop, and country to choral and chamber performances. In the past the Orpheum played host to such performers as Bob Hope, Marilyn Monroe, and Louis Armstrong; more recently, the likes of k.d. lang, Shirley Maclaine, and Jay Leno have entertained on the stage.

On your way to your next stop, walk along Granville Street and watch your feet. The BC Entertainment Hall of Fame honours British Columbia residents who have contributed to performing arts and entertainment in Canada and throughout the world by creating **Starwalk,** honorary plaques in the sidewalk along Granville Street.

The **Ford Centre for the Performing Arts** (midblock on Homer Street between Robson and Georgia Streets; for tickets call 604–280–2222) is the newest addition to the Entertainment District and was completed in 1995. This 1,849-seat theater has hosted such shows as *Showboat, Sunset Theatre, Joseph and the Amazing Technicolor Dreamcoat, and Riverdance.* From the street you can see the staircase that links the lobby levels through the large, five-story glass cone rising 82 feet over your head. The theatre entrance is at the base of the cone.

Memorabilia buffs can stop at the retail store **Showstoppers** (604–602–0616) to browse and perhaps pick up a souvenir or two. The store has music from both stage and screen musicals, as well as T-shirts, videos, and collectibles of all sorts.

Ready for a cup of coffee? Wander across the street to **Vancouver Library Square,** which houses the Public Library, along with bookstores, coffeehouses and light eating establishments. The square was designed by the same Canadian architect who devised the Ford Centre for the Performing Arts.

Next stroll over to the **Queen Elizabeth Theatre** (Georgia and Hamilton Streets; 604–665–3050; for tickets call 604–280–4444), home to the Vancouver Opera and Ballet British Columbia. The theater has been chosen for Broadway shows, and for pop and rock concerts, in addition to opera and dance. *Phantom of the Opera, Les Miserables* and *Cats,* Harry Belafonte, and David Copperfield, among others, have played to appreciative audiences at the 2,929-seat theater.

Attached to the Queen Elizabeth Theatre is the **Vancouver Playhouse** (Hamilton Street at Dunsmuir Street; 604–665–3050, for tickets call 604–280–4444). This much smaller theater, with only 673 seats, is home to the Vancouver Playhouse Theatre company (Vancouver's regional theater company), the Vancouver Recital Society, and the Friends of Chamber Music Society. More than 280 events and performances take place each year in the playhouse.

DAY ONE: EVENING
Dinner

There are a couple of truly wonderful things about the award-winning **Diva at the Met** (645 Howe Street; 604–602–7788; entrees $16 to $34). The first, of course, is that it's just downstairs from your room. What could be more convenient? But beyond that is the sheer pleasure you'll derive from the food. Executive Chef Michael Noble was a member of Canada's Culinary Olympics Team, and under his leadership the restaurant has been named by *Gourmet* magazine Top Table (1997) for Vancouver in the first year of business. When you make your early-dinner reservations, tell the staff you're going to the theater and they'll make sure you're finished in time. Beforehand allow time to linger over drinks at the bar at the entrance to the restaurant. Try a Diva Secret Passion: a smooth concoction of amber rum, vodka, peach schnapps, and passionfruit juice that's guaranteed to throw your lover into a tailspin.

The levels of the terraced restaurant are divided by exquisite etched-glass work. For more intimate dining we like the top level along the balcony. The smoked Alaskan black cod, leek whipped potatoes, celery jus, and tomato oil is the chef's signature dish and very popular with diners. The meal comes in a bowled plate, with the cod neatly arranged on the bed of creamy potatoes. The menu may change, but that dish stays. Selecting the appropriate wine for your meal is no problem, with a wine cellar that boasts 225 selections. Don't worry about rushing your meal to fit in dessert: After the theater is a grand time to have it—eliminates that hurried feeling as you try to meet the curtain call.

❦

Hotel guests attending the theater can ask to be transported there by the hotel's Jag. It's a classy way to make your entrance, so be sure to ask when you make your hotel reservations so that you can arrive in style.

After the play, with your excitement still running high, add a sugar rush and order that dessert you missed at dinner. The very rich Diva's Stilton Cheesecake with Black-Peppered Rhubarb Compote is a house specialty. If you're unable to decide, try the Diva's Dessert Platter, a selection of the most popular goodies, sinfully delicious and just begging to be shared.

DAY TWO: MORNING
Breakfast

Try a slightly different view of the city and make your way across the Cambie Street Bridge to **Remington's Restaurant** (Plaza 500 Hotel; 500 West Twelfth Avenue; 604–873–1811, $7 to $18) for brunch. Its buffet comes laden with salads, pasta, omelets, juices, roast beef, and the like, along with a full selection of desserts. You can also order a la carte, if the buffet proves more than you want to eat. Ask to sit in the bright glass atrium area; if the day is really sunny, you might want to grab a seat under one of the umbrellas there.

DAY TWO: AFTERNOON

It's your time to play around, so line up a matinee of another production for the afternoon.

FOR MORE ROMANCE

Visit during summer for the magic of the Shakespeare Festival—**Bard on the Beach** (604–739–0559)—which runs from June to late September. Bard on the Beach takes place in Vanier Park in an open-ended tent, with the sea, city, and mountains as a backdrop. This is one occasion you definitely do not want to dress up for the theater—casual and warm are the fashion directions to follow.

SPORTING CHANCE

If you've ever read a Dick Francis novel, you probably have a vivid mental picture of the excitement of a racetrack. Though there are certainly different kinds of racing, the essence is the same: hooves pounding through flying dirt; bright colors on small, monkeylike creatures clutching the backs of powerful horses; flaring nostrils and rippling flanks as horse and rider push to the limit; and, finally, the clamor of the crowd as the winner strains for the finish line.

Whether it be horses or people, the racetrack or a modern pro football game, the two of you will feel the primeval excitement of flesh-to-flesh competition that remains so alluring. The roar from thousands of throats reaches deep within you to release ancient instincts—especially with a little money riding with the jockey. The whole sporting experience is exhilarating and a ideal complement to a romantic rendezvous.

Practical notes: Football takes place in the **BC Place Stadium** (777 Pacific Boulevard; for event information and parking, call 604–661–7373, for game tickets call 604–280–4444), while the NBA's Grizzlies and the NHL's Canucks play nearby at **General Motors Place** (800 Griffiths Way, near the big dome of BC Place Stadium; for event information call 604–899–7444; for game tickets of all kinds, 604–280–4444).

MORNING

The **BC Hall of Sports Fame and Museum** (at gate A inside BC Place Stadium, 777 Pacific Boulevard; 604–687–5520; open 10:00 A.M. to 5:00 P.M.; $6.00), while not on a par with certain of the older and more extensive collections in some cities, records the achievements of both professionals and amateurs in sports in the province and is worth a visit. You'll garner a sense of the recent history of sports in the city, thus adding to your enjoyment of the rest of the day.

Romance at a Glance

♥ *Visit the BC Hall of Sports Fame and Museum (604–687–5520).*

♥ *Enjoy lunch at Courtnall's Sports Grill (604–683–7060).*

♥ *Win big on a good-looking horse at the Hastings Park Race Course (604–254–7631).*

♥ *Dine on scrumptious fare at 900 West (604–669–9378).*

♥ *Take in a professional sporting event at one of the downtown stadiums.*

AFTERNOON

Lunch

At **Courtnall's Sports Grill** (118 Robson Street, across Beatty Street from the entrance to the stadium; 604–683–7060; under $10), you can pick up a hearty lunch of burgers and pizza. Sit on the patio outside if you can, or pick any spot indoors for an unobstructed view of one of the many TVs tuned to, of course, the sports channels.

☙❧

After lunch take a flier on a red-hot tip. **Hastings Park Race Course** is Western Canada's best thoroughbred racetrack; between April and November there's always something going on, either live racing or competitions simulcast from other racecourses around the world. The track is at the **Pacific National Exhibition** (East Hastings Street, through Gate 6 off Renfrew Street or Gate 9 off McGill Street; for race days and times, call 604–254–7631; admission is $3.50 and on-site wagering on the thoroughbreds is legal). Races occur on Friday evenings and Saturday and Sunday afternoons. Visitors can also watch the mudders on Wednesday and Friday evenings for part of the summer. You can pick up race forms on-site, meander over to the paddocks where the competitors are assembling, and with a practiced eye—whether you have ever seen a horse before is irrelevant to using a practiced eye—choose a winner. Then find your way to the betting windows, be guided by those ahead of you to get the gist of wagering, and place your $2.00 bet. Once you have your receipt, select a place in the stands if it's raining or down by the rail if it's not. When the bell rings and the announcer's cadence begins to accelerate, yell like hell for your horse to come home. This is not the time for decorum; your horse needs all the help it can get to win.

EVENING
Dinner

Hoarse from an afternoon of shouting, make your way back downtown for dinner in the graceful refinement of **900 West** (Hotel Vancouver, 900 West Georgia; 604–669–9378; $16 to $28), the fine-dining restaurant on the main floor. Eating here is reminiscent of the elegant dining of the past century. From a seat in the middle of the restaurant, you'll experience the expansiveness the designers intended, and although quiet corners are usually what springs to mind when you think of romance, tonight center stage is where you want to be. The 25-foot ceilings and a semi-open plan connect the diners at 900 West to the patrons of the Lobby Bar, to new arrivals checking in, and finally to the great glass-and-brass front entrance, all visible in a peekaboo fashion from the dining room. You never feel you're off in a corner missing the excitement. All the coming and going as city businesspeople and tourists from the edge of the earth wander by does give you grist for conversation.

Still, the subtle light refracted through the wine cases seems to inspire intimate conversation, and the tables are far enough apart that you can be alone. The soft piano that entertains

Vancouver offers a sport that most other towns with professional sports franchises do not offer. Because of the mountains nearby, you can cuddle up in the cold and watch world-class ski competitions at Whistler.

both the restaurant and the Lobby Bar provides a counterpoint to the lively rumblings from next door. The service is what you'd expect from a center-of-the-city, upscale, sophisticated meeting place, and the food is delightful. Although the menu changes quarterly, the restaurant takes great pains to incorporate local bounty. Nicola Valley Venison Loin, with a bean, wild forest mushroom, and balsamic ragout; Campbell River Smoked Salmon and Trout, served with capers and dill crème fraîche; Aldergrove Yam, Potato, and Shiitake Mushroom Terrine— all are of locally harvested bounty. No need to choose a dessert—the Sampler Plate for two ($14) makes the choice for you and will fill you up with mouthwatering delicacies.

During football season you can walk from the hotel to the BC Place Stadium (about 8 blocks). GM Place is a little farther but still walkable, or take a cab.

FOR MORE ROMANCE

Most of the professional teams play on the weekend; hence, with a little judicious planning and depending on the season, you might be able to take in several games, as well as a few hours at the racetrack.

OUT AND ABOUT

LUNCH WITH THE GODS: SQUAMISH

*I*n some ways this light lunch is like standing in Chartres Cathedral or holding a baby for the first time: Everyone seems to be a bit overwhelmed at first and is completely still. Nothing prepares you for landing on a glacier and being surrounded by eternally frozen peaks. The red checks in the tablecloth are orphans in a sea of white stretching to the edges of the planet, and the air that is so pure here it squeaks as you breathe. Most surprising, it's beach-warm.

To get to your table, the ski plane flies within an arm's length of craggy snowbound peaks (not really) and sounds like it's rattling apart when ski-landing on the icefields (normal). If you breathe a little faster in small planes, close your eyes, grip your lover's hand as tight as you can, and persevere. Those blessed with flying weather dare not turn down this exclusive invitation from the gods for lunch on a glaciered peak.

Practical notes: Remember Icarus. Flights can take place only in good weather, so dowse yourself in suntan lotion or cover up. Sunglasses are a must. It could be nippy or very warm, so dress in layers. Where you're going is as close to the sun as you'll probably ever be, and it burns in no time, regardless of the season. Glacier flights run from March to mid-October, while landings and picnics take place from May to mid-October. Eagle watching is at its peak from late November to February. For the float trips you might want to take a disposable camera, which you can purchase at most drugstores, rather than your expensive gear. Take a camera and lots of film for either trip. One last but important note: The road along the cliffs of Howe Sound requires your full attention and care.

Morning

Take your time driving north to Squamish at the head of Howe Sound along the **Sea to Sky Highway** (Highway 99). Turnouts and viewing points you can use to admire the dramatic views are frequent. As you motor along, look up at the precipitous ramparts to your right. The park at **Porteau Cove Provincial Park,** about halfway up the sound (well marked in advance by signs), provides easy access to the water and view and has a restroom. Toward the back of the park along the single-lane road are walking trails leading through the picnic areas up a small hill to a prepared lookout. If you want a twenty-minute break from the drive, this would be perfect.

Romance at a Glance

♥ *Drive the cliffside road on the Sea to Sky Highway.*

♥ *Enjoy a Miner's Breakfast at the famous Ninety Niner Restaurant (604–896–2497).*

♥ *Have lunch with the gods on a glacier (800–265–0088).*

♥ *Have dinner at the Salmon House on the Hill (604–926–3212).*

♥ *Watch a thousand bald eagles watch you (604–898–1537).*

Breakfast

Some people can't walk out the door without breakfast, but if you can wait for forty-five minutes or so until you've driven up the highway from Vancouver, stop in at a British Columbia landmark, the **Ninety Niner Restaurant,** in Britannia Beach (Britannia Beach; 604–896–2497; open at 6:00 A.M.; $3 to $12). For years skiers on the way to Whistler have filled up on the Miner's breakfast, a gargantuan meal of eggs, meat, and home-made hash browns, before hitting the slopes. You can order

Reaching for You

The waters directly in front of Porteau Cove Provincial Park are home to the giant Pacific octopus, which can reach 30 feet in length according to the rangers. We don't believe any of the rumors about snacks missing from the water's-edge picnic tables (these docile creatures seem to be partial to hot dogs and ice cream, according to the stories), but double-check just to be sure before you snuggle into that arm around your shoulder.

lighter fare, such as pastries and cinnamon buns, but pancake fanatics will no doubt want to sample the flapjacks with fresh blueberries or blackberries, depending on the season.

As you approach Squamish, you'll notice a mountainous bare rock with sheer cliffs more than 2,000 feet (700 meters) high. As soon as it comes into view, slow down and look for the entrance to **Shannon Falls Provincial Park** on your right (it's well marked by highway signs). The falls are the third highest in Canada, and most people can zip right past them, because trees obscure the bottom and folks don't look up to see the top of the 335-meter (more than 1,000 feet) cascading torrent. By contrast, Niagara Falls is only 56 meters high. Stroll the short path to the base of the falls and look way up to where the waterfall seems to spring from the sky.

At Shannon every season has its special wonder. In winter the falls sometimes freeze into white lace curtains from top to bottom, while spring brings a deluge whose fine mist will soak you almost out to the parking lot. Tamer in summer and fall, Shannon cloaks itself in deep greens and blazing oranges and yellows.

A little farther on is the **Stawamus Chief,** one of Canada's premier havens for rock climbers. Rather than pulling to the side of the highway, take advantage of the parking lot at the Stawamus Chief Provincial Park about 1 kilometer beyond Shannon Falls Provincial Park. Lean way back and count the number of death-defying climbers making their way handhold by handhold up the sheer face. A good pair of binoculars will allow you to see every detail. If you feel particularly energetic and want an eagle's-eye view of Howe Sound and the Squamish Valley, make the three-hour hike to the top around the back side of the mountain. It's a steep walk, with no technical clambering at all. From the parking lot the trail is well marked.

AFTERNOON

Vancouver is the only major North American city that has glaciers within one hour of the downtown area, and other than in Alaska you'll probably never have another chance to fly in a ski-plane on this continent. **Glacier Air Tours** (Squamish Airport, Squamish; 800–265–0088 or 604–898–9016, closed mid-October to May) is British Columbia's only ski-plane company and stages out of the Squamish Airport, just north of Squamish about 8 kilometers. Turn left off Highway 99 at the sign that reads GLACIER TOURS/AIRPORT and follow the signs to the field. Call ahead both to reserve a space and to make sure it's flying weather.

Lunch

Although we fancy the alpine picnic, you can save your appetite for later and just walk around the icefields. Or take one of several sightseeing flights of the region. Each passenger has a set of headphones, and the pilots provide a trip narration of the hanging glaciers, waterfalls, alpine lakes, volcanoes, and peaks of the Tantalus Mountain Range. Prices start at $60 for an aerial tour and increase when you include a landing on one of the glaciers, a picnic or a sit-down dinner with linen and silver. The picnic flight costs $169, and the formal sit-down dinner can be as pricey as you want, depending on the number of people and the decor (candelabras, liveried servants, etc.) you want flown up. The flights range from forty-five minutes for an aerial tour to ninety minutes for a glacier picnic.

⚭

Pray for a few clouds, as they add to the dramatic contrasts and shadows on the snow white background. The pilots get a kick out of showing willing passengers their private playground, so depending on your thrill quotient, they can swoop into small alpine valleys with crystal green lakes overhung by shimmering white glaciers. These are places few ever see.

⚭

Squamish means "mother of the wind" in the tongue of the Coast Salish, and the town is named for the winds that are a normal part of every afternoon in the area. In the past few years, as windsurfing has grown popular, Squamish has become a favored destination from early spring to mid-fall, comparable to the Columbia Gorge in Oregon. To watch the windsurfers, take a walk through the trails of the **Squamish River** estuary. The estuary loop trail begins off Cleveland Avenue and is easy to find. The lazy, forty-five-minute walk is also worthwhile for the wild deer, swans, seals, and Canadian bald eagles (only the passports are different from the species that inhabits the United States) you may see along the way.

If you want to explore longer in the area, you can obtain a visitor information package in person at the counter at the Visitor Center at 37950 Cleveland Avenue. You can't miss the bright green and yellow building.

On the way back to Vancouver, stop at Britannia Beach, the site of a huge copper mine that finally played out a few years ago. If you really want to probe deeply into British Columbia history, take a tour inside the mine. The **BC Museum of Mining,** a National Historic Site, offers demonstrations of drilling and equipment between May and mid-October. (You can't miss this huge structure on Highway 99 in Britannia Beach; 604–896–2233; open 10:00 A.M. to 4:30 P.M.; $9.50 for adults and $7.50 for seniors.) The sixty-to ninety-minute tour takes you through the three-level museum and within the mountain every hour on the half-hour. Bring a jacket or a warm body, because the temperature is a constant cool 12 or so degrees centigrade (about 55 to 60 degrees Fahrenheit).

EVENING
Dinner

Time your arrival back in Vancouver for about an hour before sunset so you can watch the sun go down from the **Salmon House on the Hill** (2229 Folkestone Way, West Vancouver; 604–926–3212; reserve ahead; $15 to $24 for entrees). The menu features alder grilled salmon as the specialty. This restaurant is guaranteed to impress your lover, with its panoramic view of Vancouver, English Bay, and Vancouver Island; classy decor; and scrumptious Northwest cuisine. Don't even think of ordering steak (it's on the menu), given all the terrific seafood just waiting to slip between your lips. Everyone who comes to Vancouver orders salmon for every meal, including breakfast, and truthfully, you can't go wrong if you ask for it here. That said, you'll be missing the black-pepper-dusted tuna, served rare with wasabi cream and balsamic reduction, or the sea bass with star anise sauce. Of course, if your supper companion really loves you, he or she will let you order salmon and give you a taste of something else, right?

FOR MORE ROMANCE

Squamish is the Miami Beach of the eagle world. The word has spread through the Alaska and Northern British Columbia communities of these raptors that Squamish not only is a warm and welcoming place to spend the winter but also offers magnificent fishing. From November until February the eagles fish and frolic at their winter getaway on the Squamish River. Of course, riverside limbs are getting crowded, with several thousand eagles hanging out each winter, but if you don't mind a bit of a flap, limbs off the main drag are still easy to come by. And the people-watching is terrific. Tourists from all over the world throng the banks and float down the river.

To get to the best place to see the eagles from the banks, follow Highway 99 past downtown Squamish (past the McDonald's at the corner of the turnoff), proceed past the light at Mamquam Road, and take a left at the next light, onto Garibaldi Way. Travel about a minute to Government Road and take a right. A two-minute drive past the railway tracks brings you to the Easter Seal Camp, where you can park along the road. Cross the road and climb the dike to the viewing deck. On weekends you'll normally find volunteer interpreters here. Eagles are easily disturbed, so bring binoculars and be on the lookout for other wildlife.

Two companies offer float trips by inflatable raft down the Squamish and Cheakamus Rivers under the beaks of these hungry fishers. These are gentle one- to two-hour floats, with just a few yards of mildly bumpy water (only Class II, but thrilling). All equipment, lunch, and an interpretive guide are provided. Call **Canadian Outback Adventures** (800–565–8735; $109 per person) or **Sunwolf Outdoor Centre** (70002 Government Road, Brackendale; 604–898–1537; $79 per person, including lunch).

ITINERARY 8
Two days and one night

TRAINING FOR ROMANCE: NORTH VANCOUVER

In many ways just the thought of trains brings back romantic visions of a bygone era. For some the swaying and clicking of a train as it rolls along constitute the most soothing and relaxing form of travel. Combine such an excursion with fabulous city, water, and mountain scenery and a three-course gourmet meal, and you're in heaven.

Practical notes: Watch the weather when you dress for the train, as you will be disembarking at Porteau Cove for approximately thirty minutes. BC Rail recommends that you leave your high heels behind. The dinner train operates from May to October. Though summer is the best time to take it if you want the longest hours of daylight for the ride, we like the trip a little later in the season, so that we're still onboard when the sun sets.

DAY ONE: MORNING

Close to the Lions Gate Bridge and the narrows guarding the harbor, **Ambleside Park** in West Vancouver on the North Shore is the perfect place to watch marine traffic. Tankers, cargo ships, and luxury cruise liners on their way to or from exotic ports around the world all pass under the welcoming steel arch connecting Stanley Park to the North Shore. About half the year the foreshore next to the mouth of the Capilano River on the park's eastern boundary is filled with fishermen trying to snag the fantasy fish of their dreams. During summer families, pets, the solitary, and lovers walk its wide promenade, and the smell of coconut suntan oil and onion rings fills the air. Sunbathers crowd the sand in blissful indolence.

A slow amble along the promenade takes you westward from the park. Explore every pier. Immigrants fish and crab or use their nets on the shore to scoop smelt for Old World recipes. The city has done a superb job of creating a foreshore accessible to the public, and you can walk or run for miles with million-dollar houses on one side of the walk and the sea on the other.

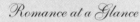

Romance at a Glance

♥ *Go for a stroll along the promenade at Ambleside Beach.*

♥ *Have a leisurely lunch at the Beach Side Café (604–925–1945).*

♥ *Unwind at Thistledown House Bed and Breakfast Inn (604–986–7173).*

♥ *Visit the salmon hatchery to see the fish climb the ladder.*

♥ *Roll along on the Pacific Starlight Dinner Train (604–984–5500 or 800–663–8238).*

DAY ONE: AFTERNOON
Lunch

The **Beach Side Café** (1362 Marine Drive, West Vancouver; 604–925–1945; $10.95 to $13.95 for entrees) is a great stopping spot for lunch. In clear weather the deck is the place to be. If you sit back from the edge a bit, you won't see the parking lot below, just the forest of Stanley Park, the sea, and the ships.

Inside the decor is soothing, with pale-colored walls and easy background music. With several French doors across the front, open in summer, even indoor seating in a light rain is romantic. The menu gives a varied selection of pasta dishes, sandwiches, salads, and the like. Absolutely save room for dessert: The Burnt Lemon Torte's silky sweetness shouldn't be missed.

❧

Thistledown House Bed and Breakfast Inn (3910 Capilano Road, North Vancouver; 604–986–7173; $110 to $189), a 1920 Arts and Crafts home, has been restored by the owners, Ruth Crameri and Rex Davidson, into a retreat from your everyday cares and worries. Whether you choose to stretch out on the wide veranda at the front or luxuriate in the soft leather furniture in the lounge, you'll love this time away.

All the rooms are showcases for the many treasures the owners have collected during their travels. Ruth's vast experience as an interior designer shows clearly throughout the house. The Inn has three guest rooms upstairs and two on the main floor at the rear. For any romantic occasion ask for the Under the Apple Tree Room, so named because it is, well, located under the embrace of a gnarled old apple tree whose scents of blossoms and fruit bless you in the morning. You won't be disappointed by this spacious yet cozy room on the main floor, with its king-size bed piled with a snowy white duvet and pillows. The tub in the bathroom is made for a soak for two. In the sunken sitting area, a love seat is nestled in front of the fireplace, surrounded by windows overlooking the garden. A door opens to the private patio just outside the suite for relaxing and enjoying the outdoors.

Across the street from Thistledown House is one of the most picturesque and romantic walks in Vancouver, down the road that veers off to the left from Capilano Road to the **Capilano Salmon Hatchery.** The hatchery is only a couple of kilometers from the sea and serves as a spawning ground for several types of salmon at certain times of the year. As you stand at the wooden rail, you'll see the fish waiting for their turn to scale the ladder to the hatchery. The hatchery exhibit is superb, with a glass wall on one side of the fish ladder so you can watch the fish doing their scales. The hatchery is open every day year-round from 8:00 A.M. to 4:00 P.M.; 4500 Capilano Park Road, North Vancouver; 604–666–1790. There is no fee.

After going through the hatchery, take a walk in the woods along the canyon. As you face the river with the hatchery on your right, take the path to your left along the excellent gravel trails. Even after a rain they are fine for all kinds of footwear, except possibly the little gold lamé sandals you were considering wearing to dinner. Take along your sneakers. Walking along the east bank, you can watch fishers standing on small cliffs and outcrops, hauling in huge salmon on their way up to spawn. From the bridge you can look upstream at the hatchery or down into the tree filtered sunlight reflecting across the river as it courses through the gorge. Cross the wooden bridge and continue along the gorge to the right. At the end of the path, as you come out of the trees, towering **Cleveland Dam** surprises you. The whole walk takes only about fifteen minutes.

For a closer look at the dam, return to your car and drive up Capilano Road for a few blocks to the entrance to Cleveland Dam, on the left. The dam provides a reservoir for much of the city's drinking water and looks down into the canyon you were in a few minutes ago.

You've crossed the canyon on a solid bridge and stood on a road across it at the dam; now dance across the water on a suspension bridge. Go back out to Capilano Road, turn right, and drive down the mountain. **Capilano Suspension Bridge** (3735 Capilano Road, North Vancouver; 604–985–7474, winter rates are $8.25 and are $1.00 higher in summer) is on the right. Parking is on the left. The bridge is a 450-foot span, 230 feet above the Capilano River. There are a series of trails around the grounds and viewing points of the river. Salmon do come upstream, and you can watch them digging in the gravel directly under the bridge. If you're lucky, you might see an eagle fishing from one of the trees along the bank.

Also worth your time here is a good historical exhibit, with lots of old pictures of the surrounding area, the park, and logging around the river. You can also sit outside with a cup of coffee on the deck overlooking the canyon or poke through the Trading Post gift shop for a wide range of goods. Although this canyon is a little more picturesque than the free one at Lynn Canyon, give it a miss during the peak summer season, when thousands of tourists swamp the area.

Tired yet? Maybe a little peckish? If it's close to 4:00 P.M., head back to the Thistledown House for afternoon tea and little downtime before getting ready to hit the rails. Though it's tempting to fill up on the homemade pastries, go lightly, as dinner is coming.

DAY ONE: EVENING

Dinner

West Coast casual is set aside tonight as you dress up in your finery and step into the past. The golden era of train travel with the white linens, 1940s Art Deco styling, and elegantly dressed passengers will be revealed to you with the **Pacific Starlight Dinner Train** (BC Rail Passenger Station at the foot of Pemberton Street, North Vancouver; 604–984–5500 or, from the United States, 800–663–8238; operates from 6:15 to 9:45 P.M. Wednesday through Sunday, May to October; $71 to $86).

Climb aboard and let the gentle swaying of the train seduce you. Smile as you enter, as a photographer will snap your photo and have it ready for you to buy as a souvenir ($10) after the ride is over. The most popular seats are those referred to as "window seats." Although there are windows on both sides of the train, only one side always has an unobstructed view of Howe Sound, while the other is up close to the side of the mountains. But with the large picture windows, we found that even those on the inside of the train can easily see the sights. If you'd like the open, airy feel of the all-glass dome car, you'll need to reserve early (up to a month in advance), as these seats are taken quickly. Keep in mind that this is the old style of train travel, where most tables are for four and on a busy evening you might well be placed with strangers for, hopefully, a little scintillating conversation. Tables for two in the dome cars are limited, so reserve early to catch one.

A three-course dinner, prepared with locally grown foods by Executive Chef Bruce Knapik, who has won awards at culinary competitions, will be served to you throughout the trip. When you make your reservation, you'll be asked to select the main course, which will be a choice of fish, beef, chicken, or vegetarian. All the wines onboard have a West Coast theme, so you'll find some of the finest from British Columbia, Washington, Oregon, and California. Try a tiny glass of British Columbia ice wine or late harvest wine to finish off your meal.

The Train May Sway You

It may be harder than you think to resist the lure the train has on your romantic soul. Within the first four months that the Starlight Dinner Train operated, many lovers succumbed and ten marriage proposals took place onboard. And even a complete wedding party was celebrated in the dome car. The marriage ceremony took place during the stopover in Porteau Cove. There is no record of any rejections, so while you have your lover on the rails, you might try to "tie" him or her up before he or she "switches"—train talk for getting hitched.

During the break at **Porteau Cove,** slip over to the gift shop on the station platform and purchase a red rose for your loved one to carry back onto the train. Also take a walk down to the water's edge. Faraway glaciers gleam golden in the fading sun if you look to the north of the fjord.

DAY TWO: MORNING
Breakfast

Drag yourselves out of bed and wander down for a scrumptious meal at the large table in the bright dining room. This is the very room where your host and hostess got married, and it's a popular spot for others to do the same.

Once seated, you could find yourselves feasting on a Portabello Mushroom Crepe with Ayrshire Bacon, a Ham and Asparagus Crepe with Chantilly Sauce, or Chicken and Mushrooms in Cream Sauce with Four-Cheese Polenta. Of course, there are also fig and anise, black olive, walnut apricot, egg twist challah, and Russian rye breads smothered in whipped sweet butter and jams or marmalades ready to be devoured.

After breakfast take your coffee outside and relax in the garden or on your private patio while you savor your brew and enjoy each other's company.

DAY TWO: AFTERNOON

We all want to feel that we're desirable, and a trip to **Rice Lake** at the right time of year can be a tremendous boost for your ego—and a warning to your mate, if he or she has been remiss, that you have certain charms others find immensely attractive. In late spring thousands of harmless dragonflies with the most iridescent blue wings are busy selecting a mate for the summer season. If you stand very still and wear anything with a lighter shade of sky blue, you'll get more gentle but ardent proposals than you can handle.

To reach Lynn Canyon valley and Rice Lake take Highway 1 east to exit 22. At the first light take a left. Just after the next light, you'll notice a blue sign that says SEYMOUR DEMONSTRATION FOREST, 5 KM, your destination. Continue on as the road narrows to a double lane, traveling through the forest, through a cemetery, and onto a well-maintained dirt road. Follow this until you reach the parking lot at the end. The lake is a short, ten-minute walk from the lot; the trip from Thistledown to the parking lot is only about twenty minutes. (To return, take the first right at the first red light and follow the signs to Highway 1 going west.)

Lunch

By midsummer this secret lake amid the mountains is bath-warm, just right for taking a swim or merely wading and feeding the ducks, so bring your suit. The path around the lake is short and easy, with detours down to the shore and connections to longer walks. Thistledown House will make you a picnic lunch if you request one, or you can pick up fixings at Lonsdale Quay on the way. Before you explore further, find a warm rock and share your feast with each other and the hungry ducklings.

⊙⊺⊙

In this valley two rivers are very close together, and you can spend the entire afternoon exploring mountain creeks. These, by the way, are snow-fed and not warm at any time of the year. Still, on hot days a dip in the cold water will revive you. From the parking lot you can walk twenty minutes through the woods to **Lynn Canyon Suspension Bridge** and the swimming hole favored by daredevils who dive from the canyon cliffs into the frigid water. (Have a look at the huge stumps of the old-growth forest cut at the turn of the century.) The creek comes out of the canyon in a lovely waterfall before it flattens into a wide, boulder-strewn stream. Try finding your way across without getting wet (or use the swinging bridge). Another alternative is to follow the trail from the parking lot toward Rice Lake and then turn off to **Lynn Creek.** At one point, about twenty minutes along, you'll come to a bridge over the river. On the opposite bank is a small museum whose offerings center on turn-of-the-century logging in the area, as well as a picturesque spot beside the rushing, clear mountain creek. As you walk, you'll notice all manner of old rusting machinery back in the bush. Some items blend in to the forest shadows so well that they're hard to spot, but you can't miss the truck chassis with the trees growing through it.

The exercise-minded can also walk, bike, or in-line skate for about 10 kilometers along the road leading to **Seymour Dam** from the Rice Lake parking lot. The road is closed to all but pedestrians and bikers on weekends and has little traffic any other time. At the end of the road is a small fish hatchery. Take the trail that leads through the hatchery into the woods. In 0.25 mile you'll come to the banks of the river and a shallow, secluded pool where you can watch the salmon jump and occasionally eagles trying their luck.

FOR MORE ROMANCE

The Pacific Starlight also runs throughout the year for special occasions such as Christmas, New Year's Eve, Valentine's Day, Easter Brunch, and Mother's Day Brunch, all with distinctive feasts.

ITINERARY 9
Two days and one night

SLIP SLIDING

*Y*ou feel a little dizzy as, arm in arm, you thread your way through the throngs on the ice. Your partner is so close that all you can see are eyes and a smile. Thrusting quickly, you match rhythms and the two of you slide down the rink. Just before reaching the end, fits of giggles interrupt any attempt at grace and you collapse against each other. Your lover's face is warm and glowing with the effort, and the diffuse light makes the person more beautiful than ever. As you start again, the ceiling twirls slowly as you make your way, thoughts of sugar and hot chocolate beginning to take hold. You guide your partner to the edge and graciously undo the skate's laces.

Practical notes: Skates can be rented for $2.00 between 10:00 A.M. and 10:00 P.M. from mid-November to March at Robson Square Skating Rink in the center of the city (800 Robson Street; 604–661–7373). Hot chocolate or wine is available from the rinkside restaurants. The rink is covered but open to the air, so you can glide even in a shower.

DAY ONE: AFTERNOON

You'll be staying in the romantic **Wedgewood Hotel** (845 Hornby Street; 604–689–7777; $160 to $540), one of Vancouver's premier boutique hotels, and as the name implies, it's luxuriously elegant. The owner, Eleni Skalbania, is well known in Vancouver as a gracious host, and this is reflected in the perfection of her creation. She and her sister, Joanna Tsaparas, are responsible for the decorating. All the wallpaper and carpets and many of the antiques are from England.

Flowers play an important part of the ambience at the Wedgewood, starting from the moment you enter the door and breathe the first scent of stargazer lilies. Any of the rooms that overlook the garden atop the law courts have special appeal, and you'll especially like the flower-stuffed window boxes on every balcony. Flowers even come with room service. All the accommodations are romantic, but if you can afford it, live a little in the Penthouse, with its own private garden terrace, wet bar, and fireplace ($250 to $540, depending on the season).

The **Vancouver Art Gallery** (750 Hornby; 604–662–4719 for exhibitions, events, and hours; closed Monday and Tuesday; $7.50 entrance fee) is Vancouver's foremost art gallery, where you are just as likely to see old masters as really offbeat exhibits from anywhere in the world. You can easily spend all day just going through the permanent collection.

Across the street and down a bit but still within sight of the Vancouver Art Gallery is **Cathedral Place** (925 West Georgia Street). Inside, hanging on the wall, is the dramatic centerpiece of the lobby, an etched-glass work by Robert Studer that resembles a navigational aid and map all rolled into one. Down the hallway to the right, past *My Honey's Buns* (another coffee shop that offers good-quality pastries and a chance to rest your feet), is the **Canadian Craft Museum** (639 Hornby Street; 604–687–8266; hours vary, depending on the season; $4.00

Romance at a Glance

♥ *Cozy into the Wedgewood Hotel (604–689–7777).*

♥ *Wander through the Vancouver Art Gallery (604–662–4719).*

♥ *Peruse the offerings at the Canadian Craft Museum (604–687–8266).*

♥ *Dine gloriously at Piccolo Mondo Ristorante (604–688–1633).*

♥ *Enjoy Venetian splendor during brunch at the Bacchus Restaurant and Lounge (604–608–5319).*

♥ *Glide at the downtown Robson Square Skating Rink (604–661–7373).*

entrance fee). It always has an eclectic collection of exhibits and complements the Vancouver Art Gallery nicely. For example, a recent exhibit was of lutes modeled on sixteenth-century Renaissance versions but constructed by local talent; soothing lute music played in the background as museum patrons perused the fourteen-course Theorbo (a large lute that accompanies tenors). In another part of the museum were exhibits of Nicole Dextras's paper casting and appliqué sculptures of people and a complete how-to course on handmaking the paper used to create her cast-paper sculptures. You're just as likely to find jewelry and metal arts or an exhibition of quilts that make a socially relevant commentary.

If you haven't been having any luck getting your special companion to relax, cross Hornby Street to the **Hong Kong Bank Building** (885 West Georgia) and go inside. The massive pendulum, all 1,600 kilograms (about 3,500 pounds) of it hangs 9 stories and does a sweep of the entire lobby every few seconds only 12 feet over your head. Drop into a seat for a cup of tea in the lobby coffee bar, **Café Ami** (885 West Georgia; 604–688–0103), and within a few minutes your mate will be as pliable as putty. When you're both properly soothed, continue on around the corner onto Howe Street. Several art galleries lie along the

2-block section heading north (toward the mountains, visible at the end of the street) from the corner of Howe and Georgia.

DAY ONE: EVENING
Dinner

To some, Venice is the most romantic city in the world. This evening, just for a little while, you will romance your loved one in a fine little restaurant in the city of canals. **Piccolo Mondo Ristorante** (850 Thurlow Street; 604–688–1633; entrees $15 to $26), only a couple of blocks from the hotel, has won numerous awards for its wine cellar. Co-owners Michele Geris and George Baugh have invested heavily to construct a list that will appeal to those who are passionate about wine. There are more than 4,000 bottles of 480 wines from all over Italy.

To complement the drink, they have also recruited two-star Michelin chef Stephane Meyer. This is Northern Italian cuisine at its finest, and the decor is distinctly fine dining. The dark green walls, hung with Italian scenes, are brightened by the blazing white of the tablecloths and the gleam of the silver. The owners are very knowledgeable about their food and wine, and they take pride in the fact that many of the ingredients they use are imported directly from Northern Italy. For a treat try the Baccala *gratinato con pinoli e sultania,* a creamy baked salt cod with pine nuts and raisins; the cod must be soaked for days to remove the salt, and the result is mouthwatering. The adventurous should order the risotto cooked with squid ink, a Venetian tradition—it's probably unlike anything you've ever eaten. Among other notable items is another exotic import from the Land of the Midnight Sun. If you're lucky enough to visit during the caribou season (approximately April until November), try a dish containing the meat, for you won't get the chance in many other restaurants. Piccolo Mondo participates in a government program that connects Inuit caribou hunters above the Arctic Circle with restaurants in lower Canada. If you like beef, you'll love caribou—it's tender and not at all gamy like some venison.

∾

Piccolo Mondo is only a block from **Robson Street,** the center of the city on a Friday or Saturday night. Street musicians, magicians, spray-paint artists, portrait sketchers, living sculptures, and mimes entertain the crowds that promenade the street. So many people come to Robson in the summer that the police filter the traffic onto the avenue to keep it moving. This is not the time to shop, since most stores, if open, are filled to the brim, but if you want to feel the pulse of the city, take a stroll down one side of Robson and then back up the other. The one exception to that might be a stop at **Lush Handmade Cosmetics** (100–1025 Robson Street; 604–687–5874). Pick up a bath bomb made with lavender or jasmine essential oils or some rose petal bath oil. We're sure you'll figure out a use for it later tonight.

Arriving back at the corner of Burrard Street and Robson, turn left for a block to the **Hotel Vancouver** (900 West Georgia; 604–684–3131), one of Vancouver's landmarks, built in the tradition of the other great Canadian Pacific Hotels, such as Lake Louise (Alberta) and the Empress (Victoria). **The Lobby Bar** (open 11:00 to 1:00 A.M.) after 9:00 P.M. should have space for you to imbibe a nightcap and listen to the live jazz. The entire lobby has recently undergone a major renovation that has given a facelift to an already popular watering hole. You'll love the huge chandeliers, wingback chairs, and genteel waiters. Drinks and snacks are at downtown-hotel prices, but the ambience is worth every penny. Grape connoisseurs should know that the bar has a good selection of wines, ports, ice wines, and so on, and the waiters can help you find something to interest your palate.

DAY TWO: MORNING
Brunch

Amble hand in hand into **Bacchus Restaurant and Lounge** (on the hotel's main floor; 604–608–5319; brunch served Saturday and Sunday from 11:00 A.M. to 2:00 P.M.; $11 to

$15). Cherrywood paneling, carved limestone fireplace, and use of gold silk and velvet are all meant to take you back to Venice in the 1930s. Cigar aficionados even have a specially constructed room where they can indulge their favorite smoke with a brandy or grappa. This is one of our favorite places, especially if we can be seated at one of the fireplace tables on a cold day. Don't get so wrapped up in each other that you don't take a look around—you never know what famous personality will drop in.

The atmosphere is intimate, the service is attentive without being a nuisance, and the a la carte menu has something for everyone. Those with a sweet tooth should order the lemon pecan blintzes with strawberry compote, some of the best blintzes we've ever eaten. On the savory side, the risotto with salmon and caviar bursts in your mouth and is one of the most popular dishes. As an alternative, the crab cakes are a seafood lover's delight, with chunks of crab and light seasoning that doesn't overwhelm the dish. The combination of crab cakes and cornbread with jalepeño peppers (not spicy) is inspired; try a bite of each separately and then together to see what we mean.

DAY TWO: AFTERNOON

The **Robson Street Skating Rink** (800 Robson Street; 604–661–7373) is a small covered area just down the steps from the art gallery in the center of everything. The Vancouver Art Gallery and Robson Street, with its upscale shopping and plethora of restaurants, are up the steps to the north side of the rink, and the law courts are up the steps to the south. The complex, designed by renowned architect Arthur Erickson, is truly unique. The law courts at the south end are roofed completely in glass, with the courts pyramided inside. The open area under the west glass is host to many of the region's more solemn ceremonies, such as the call to the bar for the annual crop of lawyers. During summer, spring, and fall, the rooftop garden of the complex is an oasis from the city (your room looks out on this garden from the Wedgewood), and the waterfall that cascades over the glass roof of the law courts muffles the sounds of the city. Be sure to go inside the government offices to the south end of the complex, to see the waterfall from below; these are the only offices in the city where the civic employees are truly underwater.

FOR MORE ROMANCE

Skating at night is different from skating during the day. Shadows soften the edges of the city and, especially in a light snow, add a magical quality. Robson Square skating is open until 10:00 P.M.

CYCLING STANLEY PARK

*N*o matter how far you cycle, be at English Bay Beach by sunset. Front-row seating isn't necessary—just grab any log and plunge your feet into the warm sand, watch the clouds above Bowen Island, and wait for the show. A blanket is a plus, because it does tend to cool off quickly as soon as the sun is gone. Later, as the moon rises, look up over your shoulder into the trees atop the bluff: Cranes surveying their domain are often silhouetted against the city lights or the lunar glow.

Practical notes: This itinerary is perfect for those long hot days of summer. If you have a pair of bike shorts with a padded seat, today is the day to haul them out. Take your swimming gear too, as you'll be passing a couple of beaches on your route and one enormous man-made pool. It's the law that you must wear a bicycle helmet when riding, and the place where you rent your bike will provide one free of charge. Make sure you do rent a bike lock, so you'll feel free to wander away from your bike. Parking can be a problem in the West End. Many streets are restricted to resident parking only, and metered spots are few and far between. We suggest making it easy on yourself by parking in the lot at the Coast Plaza at Stanley Park (1763 Comox Street; the parkade is right beside the front entrance to the hotel, a $\frac{1}{2}$ block east of Denman Street).

MORNING

Breakfast

This is not the morning to skip breakfast—you need to stoke your engines for the cycling trip ahead. If you are the muffin-and-coffee type, the **Bread Garden** (1040 Denman Street; 604–685–2996; open from 5:30 A.M. until the wee hours of the morning) should fit the bill. Or choose an almond or chocolate croissant to really make your upcoming cycle seem like a good idea. For a more substantial meal, with egg dishes, french toast or pancakes, sit outside at **Milestones** (1210 Denman Street; 604–662–3431; open from 11:00 A.M. to 10:00 P.M. weekdays and from 9:30 A.M. on weekends; approximately $8.00 for breakfast or lunch, with large portions that are easily split for two), just across from **English Bay Beach.**

❧

Bayshore Bicycle Rental—either on Denman (745 Denman Street; 604–688–2453; prices for single bikes are $5.60 per hour or $14.80 for a half-day; tandem-bike rates are $25.80 for four hours) or at the Westin Bayshore Hotel (1601 West Georgia; 604–689–5071; from March to October)—is your first stop. Both stores have free parking and are easily accessible to the park without going out onto busy streets. They also rent in-line skates. Helmets are included in the rental.

Rent a tandem or bicycle-built-for-two so you'll be able to talk and touch as you ride along. A word of warning to the person who insists on controlling the steering of the bike by riding in front: You can't tell whether or not your mate behind you is peddling. If you find yourself getting extraordinarily tired

Romance at a Glance

♥ *Have breakfast at one of the many eateries on bustling Denman Street.*

♥ *Rent a tandem bike from Bayshore Bicycle Rental (604–688–2453 or 604–689–5071).*

♥ *Visit other lovers in the aquarium (604–268–9900).*

♥ *Swill martinis at Delilah's before dinner (604–687–3424).*

♥ *Try Death by Chocolate—need more be said? (604–899–2462).*

or notice that everyone you pass is smiling at you, be suspicious that the feet behind you are resting up on the handlebars.

Regardless of the store you use, the staff can literally point you in the right direction for the **Stanley Park Seawall**—cycling on the wall is allowed only in a counterclockwise direction on designated paths or on roadways. The people at Bayshore Bicycle Rental will give you a map to help you on your way.

This is the day for a leisurely cycle. The trip along the perimeter seawall is a relaxed 10 kilometers (about 6 miles) and can be cycled in less than an hour. But you'll miss some of the best the park has to offer if you don't stop along the way to wander the beaches, admire the **Lions Gate Bridge,** stand in awe of the totem poles, and enjoy the birds at **Lost Lagoon.** You can also go off the seawall to explore the park's forest trails. When you include the interior trails, you can spend all morning cycling the park's 1,000 acres.

AFTERNOON
Lunch

You can collect a healthy lunch to take along with you from the numerous vegetable and fruit markets along Denman Street, or buy a sandwich at the Bread Garden to take out. Either way, supplement your meal with a cool drink and feed each other an order of greasy fries— loaded with flavor—from the concession stand on **Third Beach.** These are reputed to be the best fries in the city, and you can justify the calories by cycling another hour or two.

ᦗ

After you return your bikes, visit the **Vancouver Aquarium** (Stanley Park; 604–268–9900; open 10:00 A.M. to 5:30 P.M.; $10.00 for adults and $8.75 seniors) for the afternoon. It's within walking distance of the bike shop, or you can drive over (parking for the whole day is only $3.00). With 8,000 live animals—from anacondas to otters—the various galleries will give you a view of life in different parts of the world. The Arctic Canada exhibit will show you beluga whales, the Pacific Northwest exhibit has sea otters and killer whales, the Tropical Pacific Gallery has divers swimming with blacktip reef sharks, and the Amazon Rain forest has a rainstorm every hour so that you can watch how the tropical animals react to a storm. Just don't spend too much time around the sloths snoozing in the rainforest—it may give you nap ideas.

In addition, training sessions with killer whales and dolphins are held several times a day in the main pool. Prepare to get wet if you sit in the front rows. The whales love soaking the spectators by launching themselves high in the air and then flopping on their sides. They've never quite emptied the pool doing this, but they always try. The underwater viewing ports will also give you a spectacular look at the animals underwater as they work with the trainers.

EVENING
Dinner

Cuddling into a booth at **Delilah's** (1789 Comox Street at the corner of Denman; 604–687–3424; $18.50 for a smaller dinner and $29.00 for a full dinner) is only half the fun. This is known around town as the restaurant that brought back the martini. We recommend the Metropolitan (with a touch of fruit and cranberry) for beginners. Nondrinkers can have a Virgin Metropolitan, which is tasty and doesn't dull the senses for the feast to come.

This restaurant is a favorite among the West End crowd, and you can either go early (5:30 to 6:30 P.M.) or stand in line. Reservations are only for crowds of six or more. The wait is worth it. Dark, candlelit, red-velvet booths and armchairs at the tables, tons of fresh flowers, and gooseneck sconces around the room set the scene.

Eat a light dinner, with your choice of soup, salad, or appetizer plus an entree, or the full dinner of soup, salad, appetizer, entree, and dessert. We love the house specialty, Fresh Australian Rack of Lamb done Szechwan-style ($6.50 extra charge).

♥ *From Kits Point*

♥ *From Cloud Nine revolving restaurant (604–687–0511)*

♥ *From the Salmon House on the Hill restaurant (604–926–3212)*

♥ *From the top of Grouse Mountain*

♥ *From the deck of a sailboat in the bay*

Our choice is to eat a light dinner and head along the block to Death by Chocolate for dessert. Of course, those with a sweet tooth may not have a problem eating dessert in both places. Or share one at each location.

When you exit Delilah's on Comox Street, turn right and proceed to Denman Street. On Denman turn right and walk along to the next corner (Nelson Street), where you'll see your next stop across the street: **Death by Chocolate** (1001 Denman Street; 604–899–2462; open until midnight weekdays and until 1:00 A.M. weekends; $6.95 to $14.95). Once you've placed your order, the staff will invite you to watch them design your dessert.

To make it really easy for you to decide, the menu is a binder of photographs of the desserts for you to choose from. With names like French Affair, Hot and Sticky, Skinny Dip, Between the Sheets, and, of course, Death by Chocolate, you'll be sure to find something to tickle your taste buds.

Wipe the chocolate from your faces—the evening is not over yet. Take a slow walk along Denman Street to English Bay and indulge in a little people-watching. At **English Bay Beach** grab a log and settle in for the setting of the sun.

FOR MORE ROMANCE

For the illusion of seclusion, try Third Beach. The way it's positioned, out on the point of the Stanley Park Peninsula, Vancouver disappears behind the trees. Fishing atop the rocks or in the trees behind you there are always long-legged blue herons.

RIVER RAPTURE: NEW WESTMINSTER

*D*o the opening stanzas of "Old Man River" give you goose bumps? Do you play CDs of the sounds of running streams instead of music? If so, you'll love the Fraser River waterfront. The river is one of North America's largest and over the years has been a major highway for traders, fishermen, pioneers, prospectors, gold miners and other adventurers.

So much is going on now that some people sit all day just watching—tugs hauling gargantuan log booms to the sea, steel-hulled fishing boats cruising home with their day's catch, pleasure boaters out for joyrides, huge container ships dropping off another week's supply of new cars, and thousands of returning salmon persistently trying to avoid everything and get on with the job of procreating. Old-fashioned paddlewheelers transport tourists, and a recently decommissioned Soviet Foxtrot submarine attracts the curious to the rails of the New Westminster Quay. The air smells sweetly of freshly cut fir sap from the sawmills operating nearby and freshly baked bread from the market. Go and absorb it.

Practical notes: If you're driving, head out Kingsway forever. It turns into Twelfth Street within the boundary of New Westminster. Follow it to the bottom T junction at Stewardson Way. Take a left and watch for the market on your right, at the foot of Eighth Street. This itinerary works best on a weekend from late spring to September or early October. With slight modification it will work during the week too.

DAY ONE: MORNING

Drop your bag at the **Inn at Westminster Quay** (900 Quayside Drive, New Westminster; 800–663–2001; $150 to $195). If the hotel is too full to allow early check-in, the staff will store your bags until later.

Romance at a Glance

♥ *Settle in at the Inn at Westminster Quay (800–663–2001).*

♥ *Dream from the deck of a old-time paddlewheeler (604–525–4465).*

♥ *Visit Fort Langley National Historic Site (604–888–4424).*

♥ *Try a little French at Restaurant des Gitans (604–524–6122).*

♥ *Exercise your laugh lines at Lafflines Comedy Club (604–525–2262).*

♥ *Do brunch at the Boathouse overlooking the water (604–525–3474).*

Along the waterfront near the hotel is a paddlewheeler permanently tied up at the dock: the ***Samson V* Maritime Museum** (604–522–6894; closed December to March; entrance fee is by donation). This is the last of five *Samsons* built that have worked the river and the last of hundreds of paddlewheelers on the river. The first *Samson* was built in 1884, and the current model was launched in 1937. You can't help but imagine yourself a pioneer when you visit the engine paces and bridge.

After the museum hurry on down the wharf just past the market to the *Native,* another sternwheeler built in 1985 but based on a nineteenth-century design. **Fraser River Connection** (604–525–4465; open summers and Christmas; departs at 10:00 A.M.; sunset cruises on Friday and Saturday; reservations recommended), the owner of the ship, runs paddlewheeler cruises from Westminster Quay up the Fraser River past Barnston Island and Port Hammond to the village of Fort Langley, the birthplace of British Columbia. For $54 you can take a seven-hour, narrated historical tour that runs along the river and includes a buffet lunch. The boat docks for ninety minutes at Fort Langley, long enough to give you a feel for the life of the first settlers at the fort or to explore the village.

Elevate Your Love

Some visitors prefer to stay in the hubbub of downtown Vancouver rather than in New Westminster and travel out to visit the river. From downtown you can take your car or use the SkyTrain ($2.25 one-way with on-and-off privileges for ninety minutes), which will drop you exactly where you want to be. Besides freeing you from fighting traffic or looking for a parking space, the train is elevated all the way and will give you a look at several Vancouver neighborhoods en route. Service is frequent, and the mode takes about as long as driving. Get on at any SkyTrain stop and head east to the New Westminster stop. The Westminster Quay Public Market is right outside the gates of the station. Just head toward the water.

Fort Langley National Historic Site (23433 Mavis Avenue, Fort Langley; 604–888–4424; open 10:00 A.M. to 5:00 P.M. daily; $4.00 admission) was originally a Hudson's Bay Company trading post and has now been restored. The original storehouse still exists, and several reconstructed buildings are here. Men and women in period costumes give interpretive talks and demonstrate the myriad skills needed on the frontier. The Big House is where the Colony of British Columbia was proclaimed in 1858.

The rural village itself offers numerous restaurants, antiques shops, and artist's studios to peruse. If forts and shops don't make your heart flutter, walk down Main Street to the cemetery. Generations of pioneer families are buried together here, and when you read the inscriptions and dates, you can't help but imagine what life would have been like for the two of you. If you'd rather walk than explore, go down to the river road behind the fort and walk along the river. Some of the most pastoral settings in the province are in this area. With a bit of cloud and sun to soften the light, the purple Coast Mountains in the background, and the river gently flowing past, you'll see what drew civilized people from Europe to endure the rough life of the coastal rainforests.

DAY ONE: EVENING

The boat docks back at 5:00 P.M. and you'll be hungry. Check into your room and change for dinner. The inn has several rooms built out over the river (it gives new meaning to sleeping with the fishes), and although all the rooms have an unobstructed view of the river, our favorites are Bridal Jacuzzi Suites 325, 425, or 525. They each have balconies that open onto the river, and through the front picture window you get an expansive view of the waterfront. (Just don't forget your bathrobe if you leave the curtains open, or the crowds on the waterfront in the morning will have an expansive view of you.) At night the warning lights of the two bridges in the distance, the greens and reds of the water traffic, and the dim quay make it a bit like gazing at a twinkling fairyland. The rooms are sumptuous, with dark woods and thick Belgian-style carpets, and although we'd prefer that the double Jacuzzi had a view of the river (and the people in the river are glad it doesn't), it makes up in its size what it lacks in its view. The exercise-minded can take advantage of the inn's exercise room, which does offer a view: In addition to the latest equipment, the room features one whole wall looking out onto the river.

Dinner

For dinner take a short walk to the **Restaurant des Gitans** (389 Columbia at Fourth, New Westminster; 604–524–6122; $18 to $26 for entrees). The menu changes almost nightly but usually has classic French preparations of beef, pork, venison, and a few seafood dishes. On weekends the restaurant features live jazz, and the service is attentive anytime. Reservations are a must.

⊙⊕⊙

After dinner cross the street to **Lafflines Comedy Club** (26 Fourth Street, at Fourth and Columbia; 604–525–2262; $6 on Thursday and $10 on Friday and Saturday) for an evening of belly laughs. Reservations are necessary (you probably won't get in without one) for the 9:30 P.M. show.

DAY TWO: MORNING
Brunch

Stretch out and relax for a while—there's no serious touring to do today. Instead order a little coffee from room service, and when you're ready, walk down to the market. If you go around opening time (hours are 9:30 A.M. to 6:30 P.M. for all merchants in the market), you'll have your choice of hot croissants just seconds out of the oven, doughnuts dripping hot sugar, newly dressed bagels, and a lake of exotic coffees from places you never had the money to visit. Buy a newspaper from the wide selection at **Cody Books Ltd.** upstairs in the market (for those of you who can't live without *The New York Times* Sunday edition, Cody's has it), purchase a ginger blossom or a rose from the florist near the east door (Quay West Flowers; 604–520–1307) for your table, and find a seat in the dining area by the riverfront, inside or out. As an alternative, the **Boathouse** (next to the Inn at Westminster Quay; 604–525–3474, open from 8:30 A.M. on Sunday and earlier on other days) has a wide selection of more traditional morning fare, such as omelets, cereal, and croissants for $8.95, and a terrific view of the river. An attentive staff means you don't have to hunt for your own breakfast and can sit quietly until the first cappuccino is delivered to your table. (Sit outside if you can.) Since the restaurant is connected to the inn, you can even wear your bedroom slippers. Later risers can stuff themselves between 10:00 A.M. and 2:00 P.M. on the tantalizing full brunch, which features crepes, eggs Benedict, salads, seafood, stir-fries, fruit, pastries, pastas, and, for chocoholics, chocolate fondue. The cost is $15.95.

❧

After breakfast explore the market, which boasts everything from bookstores to clothiers to art galleries. And just out front and to your left is a burgeoning antiques row, along Front Street, where you'll find everything from a full dining room suite of Queen Anne furniture to 1950s bric-a-brac you'll remember from your relative's house. Much of the furniture is from England, either imported over the years or brought by Europeans who have moved here, but there is also a smattering of Canadiana, roughly cut plank-and-board country furniture from the late 1800s and 1900s. Watercolors and oils that are by local artists of little renown but show off the recognizable landmarks around Vancouver hang on the walls and are inexpensive historical mementos of the area.

DAY TWO: AFTERNOON

How close do you really want to be? The Soviet U–521 Foxtrot sub **Russian Submarine BC Ltd.** (604–520–1073; open 9:30 A.M. to 6:30 P.M. daily; $7.49), parked alongside the quay, was in operation with the Soviet Navy until recently. History buffs get a charge out of the tour of the cramped quarters that hosted crews for up to several months at a time. The kitchen was so tiny that cooks had to be under 5 feet standing up to do the work of feeding seventy-five men three meals a day. No matter how much of a history buff you are, everyone is pleased to be back on the dock.

FOR MORE ROMANCE

Sopressata Calabrese, Friulano salami, and white Stilton with ginger—the New Westminster Quay is a terrific place to put together an impromptu picnic lunch. We

New Life for Old Man River

The **New Westminster Quay** was an effort by city fathers to revitalize the riverfront district of British Columbia's oldest city (founded in 1859). The city, named by Queen Victoria, eventually became moribund and the waterfront crowded by industrial activity, decidedly not the kind of place to bring your lover for a quiet walk along the river. In the past fifteen years, however, farsighted souls have developed the quay as the centerpiece of a redevelopment project that has blossomed. Now the area is up and coming, with new high-rise luxury apartments touting their views of the river and mountains (Mount Baker, in Washington State, a classic snowcovered volcano cone, stands out from the purple mountain background from condos on upper floors).

recommend trying some of the exotic cheeses and salamis at **Cheese Please Plus** (110–810 Quayside Drive, New Westminster; 604–520–5092). James and Anne Auld will make suggestions and let you sample. Next door is a bakery for a fresh French baguette or a loaf of sourdough, and down a stall or two is all the fresh fruit you could ever want from all over the world. Either use the tables out front (inside if it's raining) or travel down the quay to a quiet bench overlooking the water.

ITINERARY 12
Two days and one night

REACHING THE PEAKS:
THE NORTH SHORE MOUNTAINS

*V*ery few places in the world are blessed with accessible mountain peaks overlooking the city. Vancouver has been given three mountains with incomparable views of the city and the surrounding Coast Mountains marching to the horizon. Each of the three offers a completely different experience, from the elegant to the sublime, and holds a special allure for lovers.

Practical notes: Each of the mountains is a year-round playground. Except for midsummer, take along extra clothing regardless of which mountain you go to. Mountain air tends to be cooler and windier and you'll be more exposed to the sun than at lower elevations. At an average 3,700 feet above sea level, Slip (on a shirt), Slap (on a hat), and Slop (on thirty-plus SPF suntan lotion), especially if you're going to the "Cypress Beach" party in the spring. Each mountain also has facilities that rent skis and other equipment. Take a pair of binoculars and your camera—even to dinner.

DAY ONE: MORNING

For your skiing escape check into the **Ocean Breeze Bed and Breakfast** (462 East First Street, North Vancouver; 604–988–0546 or 800–567–5171; from $110). The cheerful peach-, white-, and green-colored gingerbread house is well located for easy access to each of the ski mountains. You'll generally find an intriguing mix of guests from around the world to visit with in the lounge or at breakfast, and the owner, Margaret Gradowska, a former flight attendant, knows a lot about making people feel at home and looking after their needs. Ask for the Eagle's Nest when you reserve—it takes up the entire top floor of the house. The richly tiled bathroom has a big soaker tub and a view of the city.

Your first stop is **Cypress Bowl Provincial Park,** for either downhill or cross-country skiing. Take Highway 1 west toward Horseshoe Bay. Watch for the exit sign for the Provincial Park and Ski Area. Just follow the road up the switchbacks all the way to the top. About halfway up the mountain is a lookout that offers one of the best views of the city, Fraser Valley, the islands, and the Strait of Georgia. At the top a major paved road veers off to the right. Straight ahead is **Cypress Bowl** (604–926–5612), the downhill ski area. Continuing along the road to the right, you'll see the ticket and rental offices and parking for the cross-country trails.

The cross-country ski section (604–922–0825; open 8:30 A.M. to 10:00 P.M.; $10.50 for all day and $8.50 for just the evening ski session) is fairly flat and easy, with a few minor exceptions, and is a great place to try the sport for the first time. Passersby are always helpful, and you can count on impromptu lessons if you ask. At the very least the two of you will enjoy the fresh mountain air among the snow-laden trees and have a few laughs. When you need a snack and some hot chocolate, **Hollyburn Lodge** (604–922–2887; open only in winter; $3.00 to $5.00) is a rustic cafe out in the woods that you can reach only by skis or snowshoe. Yummy hot chocolate, soups and

Romance at a Glance

♥ *Stay at the Ocean Breeze Bed and Breakfast (604–988–0546).*

♥ *Cross-country or downhill ski at Cypress Bowl Provincial Park (604–922–0825).*

♥ *Snack in the snowy woods at Hollyburn Lodge (604–922–2887).*

♥ *Eat at the Grouse Nest and night ski if you have the legs (604–984–0661).*

♥ *Ski at Mount Seymour for an easy day (604–986–2261).*

chowders, and an array of sandwiches are available and, when taken with a little frosty air and mountain sunshine, are exquisite.

The most romantic place on the mountain is at the very top of the downhill ski area, where you can look out over the snowcapped Coast Mountains all the way to the horizon. It takes two chairlifts to get to the peak (open 8:30 A.M. weekdays and 8:00 A.M. weekends to 11:00 P.M.; $28 for a part-day lift ticket and $33 for a full-day ticket), but the view on the way up of the Gulf Islands and Vancouver is spectacular. Once at the peak, walk straight ahead to the edge of the cliff overlooking Howe Sound, Bowen Island, and the Sunshine Coast just beyond Bowen. On a clear day you can see south to the United States, the Olympic Peninsula, and Mount Baker (Washington State's dormant volcano).

Lunch

There's a cafeteria on the hill, but in good weather during the several weeks of spring skiing, cooks sometimes charbroil hamburger and hot dogs free of charge for anyone who goes to the very top. Charbroiled hamburgers have the unusual property of tasting better the higher you go, and these deserve only the highest accolades. Nothing beats hanging around in the sun and the snow to feed the birds just beginning to venture out after a tough winter and to watch the trees unburden themselves of ice one sparkling drop at a time.

❀

DAY ONE: EVENING
Dinner

Leave yourself time for a refreshing nap before dinner. There's still lots to see, and if you have legs left, you can still do a bit of night skiing or skating at the Peak of Vancouver. After dressing for dinner (casual), drive along Capilano Road all the way to

Cypress Beach

If you and your lover are happiest basking in the sun and lazing away the day reading and napping, **Cypress Beach** *is the earliest opening of a beach in Canada—or north of Florida and Southern California, for that matter. In the early spring—late March or April, depending on the weather— sunbathers begin arriving at Cypress Beach along the road between the downhill and cross-country areas. Since the snow is several feet deep on the slopes side of the road, partygoers dig flat areas back into the embankment of snow. The sides provide protection from the wind and reflect the sun into the interior. With lawn chairs, bathing suits, and libations of all kinds (it's illegal to drink alcoholic beverages in public, and the area is patrolled), early tanners set to work improving their complexion. Be aware that higher altitude and reflecting snow will crisp you in just a few minutes; deep frying takes only a few minutes more, especially if you have basted properly.*

Over the years the informal gathering—sometimes hundreds of the sun-starved gather on the slopes—has gained momentum, and it's now an official "beach" for a month or so every spring. The ski hill runs advertisements inviting the winter-worn to come sample the sun. The result is the incongruous sight of skiers with every square inch of exposed flesh covered standing next to near-naked sunbathers in several feet of snow.

the top. **Grouse Mountain Resort** (6400 Nancy Green Way; 604–984–0661, complimentary Sky Ride if you have confirmed reservations at the Grouse Nest or $16 if you do not) is at the top of Capilano Road, which confusingly turns into Nancy Green Way halfway up. Once you park or disembark, ride the aerial tram to the resort at the top of the mountain. One of the restaurants there, the **Grouse Nest** (604–984–0661; $17 and $24 for entrees), offers fine dining based on West Coast cuisine and a stunning view of the nighttime city. The place is popular, so reserve ahead, especially on weekends.

Although all the tables in the Grouse Nest have a view, the most romantic tables are numbers 4 and 5, at the point of the restaurant. Each table seats only a couple, and because the tables are situated at a point of the room built out over the mountain and you face away from the rest of the restaurant, it seems that you're alone. One look over your shoulder at all the interested faces peering at the view, however, will remind you to keep your hands above the table. The restaurant will not reserve window tables, which are much in demand, but you can request one, and if you arrive early by a half-hour or so, chances are good that you'll be able to swing a window seat. While you're waiting, you can sit in front of the huge stone hearth inside the front door of the lodge on the main level. The varnished log interior and log carvings are exactly what you would expect in an alpine lodge at any world-class resort miles from the nearest city.

Also while you wait, watch the half-hour, high-definition digital movie at the **Theater in the Sky.** It's included in the price of your Sky Ride ticket and takes you on a tour of British Columbia, emphasizing the natural beauty of the province. The aerial videos will show you parts of the province most natives never get to see. The picture gallery in the lobby and exit of the theater are worth a few minutes too.

For dinner we especially recommend the wild mushroom and leek ravioli in pesto cream as an appetizer. The large ravioli are enough for two of you to share. We highly recommend the West Coast Cioppino as an entree. Chunks of fresh fish, mussels, crab, prawns, clams, and scallops are blended in a full-flavored tomato Pernod broth that is one of the best bouill-abaisses in Vancouver. The rich risotto with sun-dried tomatoes is also definitely worth the calories, and the clam chowder has won awards.

❧

Be sure to leave time to walk around outside. Grouse has progressed over the years from a log cabin to a whole complex that has something to offer regardless of the time of year you visit. Local chainsaw artist Glenn Greensides has produced heroic sixteen-foot sculptures of the forest—including grizzlies, wolves, and loggers—that are a marvel. During summer the Logger Sports Shows—high-speed chopping and splitting competitions by local Paul Bunyans—merit a look.

If you arrive before sundown and it's warm enough, you might want to relax on the deck for a bit and take in the ambience of the ski resort. Or take a tour on the sleigh. The rides pulled by a tracked Sno-Cat make a circuit every half-hour and take you across the ski slopes and through the woods. To put a little thrill in your love life, try a kiss during a helicopter tour from the mountaintop helipad. Tandem paragliding is offered during some seasons and weather permitting, for those who need a death-defying act to jump-start their romance. (Call Grouse Mountain at 604–984–0661 for information.)

There are, of course, downhill skiing, snowboarding, cross-country skiing, and snowshoeing. Night skiing goes on until 11:00 P.M. and is a whole different experience from skiing during the day. The starkness of the light, the changing shadows as you cruise the slopes, and the descent toward the twinkling city lights below are something you're unlikely to experience anywhere else in North America. An added attraction: the dark spots to sneak kisses on some of the trails. Or you and your sweetie can try the new skating pond, open from 9:00 A.M. to 10:00 P.M. (skate rentals are available).

DAY TWO: MORNING
Breakfast

Breakfast is created with a flourish by Richard, the chef, downstairs in the sun-washed, open-plan kitchen and dining area. Get there early and you can grab one of the choice spots at the counter and watch Richard entertain you as he cooks up an imaginative spread. You may drool over Vanilla French Toast, stuffed with bananas and nuts and smothered with strawberry sauce, or French Parfait, with caramelized bananas. Whatever's on the menu, you won't go away hungry and probably won't need lunch.

❦

Mount Seymour (1700 Mount Seymour Road, North Vancouver; 604–986–2261) smells the best. The tang of fir trees in the air is so thick that it will have you licking your lips in anticipation. This mountain is a little less challenging than the other two mountains for downhill skiing and is perfect for beginners. In summer hiking to the top of the mountain from the parking lot along ski trails is popular (allow two to three hours for the hike). You can spend the day gorging on wild blueberries and peering over the cliffsides at Indian Arm, another fjord branching from the main Vancouver Harbor channel. Off in the distance are Mount Baker and the whole Fraser River Valley.

FOR MORE ROMANCE

Inspiring envy is neither romantic nor seemly, but once in a while it's a thrill to indulge your baser side. Vancouverites do it all the time in the early spring. Here's how to do it well: On a sunny day spend the early part of the day spring skiing. Have lunch at the top and then spend the afternoon sailing in the bay. (For boating charters, day sails, powerboat, or seadoo rentals, look in the Yellow Pages under "Boat.") Just before going into dinner at one of the seaside cafes on Denman Street, call one of your friends back east and just slip into the conversation what you did for the day. It drives the snowbound wild, and your friends might not speak to you for days.

ONCE UPON A TIME

ITINERARY 13
Two days and one night

LOOKING BACK: HISTORIC VANCOUVER

*I*f you're like us, you gravitate to the oldest section of each new city you visit. Somehow the fascination of knowing where a city began helps you appreciate where it now is. As you look at the city of Vancouver, imagine back only a century, when just about everything around you was forest. Sailing ships still pulled into the bay, and the center of the province was New Westminster or Victoria. "Gassy Jack" Deighton, quite a talker by all accounts and in whose honor Gastown was named, built his saloon at the corner of Water Street and Carroll across the railway tracks from the Hastings Mill, then at the foot of Main Street. Within a few years other buildings followed and the first settlement on the downtown peninsula was under way. Today you both will enjoy the variety and bustle of this part of the city. It has something for everyone. From souvenir shops to serious antique buying, from inspiring views to unhurried meals served in a quiet corner while you watch the harbor lights, Gastown can engage your romantic souls.

Practical notes: This itinerary is best done during the tourist season (May to early October), because many of the city tours and the trolley rides are seasonal. If you're visiting on a weekend, please note that "O Canada" House generally has a minimum two-night stay.

DAY ONE: AFTERNOON

Romance at a Glance

♥ *Stay at "O Canada" House (604–688–0555).*

♥ *Enjoy the view during lunch at the Prow Restaurant (604–684–1339).*

♥ *Take a Historic Walking Tour of Gastown (604–683–5650).*

♥ *Dine at the Raintree at the Landing (604–688–5570).*

♥ *Have an after-dinner drink at the Steamworks Brewing Company (604–689–2739).*

♥ *Take a trolley ride around the city with the Vancouver Trolley Company (604–451–5581 or 888–451–5581).*

What a perfect place to stay for a historic look at the city! It was at **"O Canada" House** (1114 Barclay Street; 604–688–0555; $125 to $195) that the Buchan version of Canada's national anthem, "O Canada," was written in 1909. This 1897 Victorian house, in the heart of Vancouver's West End, was on the point of being torn down when the new owners, Jim Britten and Mike Browne, bought it and renovated it for use as a B&B. That they've done a good job is evidenced by the top-ranking City of Vancouver Heritage Award they received.

Several nice aspects of "O Canada" House make it more like an inn than a B&B. Virtually the whole of the main floor and all of the top two floors, where the bedrooms are, are given over to guest use. Two adjacent, antique-laden parlors with fireplaces are on the main floor, as is a bright dining room. Off the dining room is a pantry outfitted with coffee, tea, juices, and freshly baked goods, available for you twenty-four hours a day whenever the munchies move you.

The guest rooms are each cozily decorated in warm taupes, soft creams, and plenty of antiques. Look carefully at the pictures on the walls to see if you can figure out which ones are of Vancouver a little more than a century ago. (*Hint:* The downtown waterfront was mostly tall trees.) All the rooms have private bath, and the VCR, telephone, and fridge are placed discretely to blend in with the decor. The telephones, although push-button, are replicas of an older style and look as if they truly belong. In the main house are five guest rooms, including the top-floor Penthouse, which stretches the whole length of the house and is furnished with two queen-size beds and a couple of cushioned benches in the dormer at the front of the house. For an extra feeling of privacy, ask for the separate cottage in the back of the main house, with its own fenced-in, foliage-surrounded patio.

Most appealing to us is the North Suite, at the front. It stretches the width of the house and has a large bay window, a king-size bed, two comfy armchairs, and, in the spacious bathroom, a wonderful clawfoot tub (with shower). In this as in all the other rooms, a soft brown fuzzy stuffed moose is sitting on the bed to welcome you when you enter.

Lunch

Leave your car behind at the "O Canada" House (free parking is in the back of the building) and walk to the **Prow Restaurant** in the Canada Place building (at the end of the pier of Canada Place, 999 Canada Place Way; 604–684–1339; open 11:30 A.M. to 2:30 P.M.; $9 to $15 for luncheon entrees; call for dinner reservations and information). The 20-block walk takes you through the heart of downtown. Or you can take your car and get two hours of free parking at the restaurant, but if you want to leave your car there while you tour Gastown, it's expensive. A cab might be a better bet.

When you reach the front door of Canada Place, veer to your left and walk to the end of the promenade. During the cruise season you're likely to see one or more large luxury ships—preparing for a weekly voyage to Alaska—berthed on your left as you walk along outside or inside the glass-enclosed promenade. At the far end of the building, the walkway will curve away to your right and you'll see the Prow Restaurant. (If you take your car, enter the underground parking off Howe Street and drive to the back of the parking lot; then take the elevator up to the restaurant floor as marked.)

The Prow is the restaurant we always take visitors to, whether for lunch or dinner. The seating is virtually surrounded with windows, and the clever placement of mirrors extends the outside images and gives the illusion of being perched over the water. Watch for the SeaBus traveling back and forth from the terminal next door to the North Shore and the float planes landing nearby. The menu at the Prow Restaurant features a range of choices, from peppered linguine with prawns to beef tenderloin stir-fry to Dungeness crab and live lobster fresh from a flight from Nova Scotia. Linger a while and delight in each other's company as you share one of the sinfully rich desserts, arguably among the best in the city. The walk this afternoon should work off some of the calories.

ଚ∘ତ

At the end of your meal, walk back to the front of the building and turn left. You might take a moment to peek at the **Pan Pacific Hotel** (999 Canada Place Way; 604–662–8111) lobby up the main escalator as you pass. The interior waterfall has been known to impress even the jaded, and from the outdoor seating just beyond the lobby, you can look closely at the sails atop the building. A quiet piano lounge with a view of the seaplane harbor and cruise ships sits off to the left; called the **Cascades Lounge** (999 Canada Place Way; 604–662–8111), it's a good spot for a drink or a cup of afternoon tea.

Back out the front door, continue left until you reach the stoplight at the corner of Howe and Cordova Streets and again turn left. As you walk downhill, you'll cross under a walkway inscribed GATEWAY TO HISTORIC GASTOWN. Just beyond this, on your left, is the **SkyTrain and SeaBus Terminal.** This restored, white-columned, red-brick building was previously the Canadian Pacific Railway Station, where passenger trains arrived from across Canada until the 1970s. Now it houses both the downtown terminus of the SkyTrain, the city's elevated rapid transit system, and the SeaBus, also part of the transit system to the North Shore.

Across the street is Harbour Centre Tower, a tall building with a round top. Inside a glass elevator takes you to an observation deck that many first-timers to the city use to orient themselves. The **Lookout** (555 West Hastings Street; 604–689–0421) is open all year (8:30 A.M. to 10:30 P.M. in summer and 10:00 A.M. to 9:00 P.M. in winter) and costs $8.00 for adults for unlimited rides all day.

Just past the parking lot next to the terminal is the beginning of Water Street, angling off to the left. You'll be able to tell you're there by the brick road, the old-style lampposts, the many trees that are lit up at night, and the wildly colored hanging baskets.

There are numerous shops and galleries to visit as you stroll along, but don't miss looking at the architecture and interesting nooks and crannies of the area. Along the friezes of some of the buildings are the carved faces of several Gastown building owners who still work and lunch in the area, so don't be surprised if you spot a familiar face ducking into a doorway. Although some shops sell typical trashy tourist T-shirts, many merchants have been in the area for years and sell unique and interesting merchandise. As just one example, even if you are not an art aficionado, you won't want to leave Vancouver without examining quality genuine Inuit and Northwest Coast Native masks, jewelry, wood and bone carvings, and other art. The **Inuit Gallery of Vancouver Ltd.** (345 Water Street; 604–688–7323) and **Hill's Indian Crafts** (165 Water Street; 604–685–4249; open 9:00 A.M. to 9:00 P.M.), where President Bill Clinton shopped for family Christmas gifts in 1997, will give you a good idea if you want to see more.

To get the entire scoop on Gastown, you can take a **Historic Walking Tour of Gastown** (604–683–5650; June through August; ninety minutes' duration; departing from Maple Leaf Square at the "Gassy Jack" statue at 2:00 P.M. daily). If you'd rather discover on your own, here are a few places not to miss: Walking down the left-hand side of Water Street, you'll run into a crowd gathered about the **Steam Clock** at the corner of Cambie and Water Streets. It's the last remaining steam clock in the world, and to the delight of crowds who are willing to suffer rain, snow, and elbowing masses, it blows steam every hour and plays a hot little tune every fifteen minutes.

Water Street is only about 3 blocks long, and at the end is **Maple Leaf Square,** formed by the junction of Carrall, Powell, and Alexander Streets. There you'll see the proud figure of "Gassy Jack" atop a barrel. Across the street is the former **Europe Hotel,** one of Vancouver's most elegant properties when it was first built in 1908. The builder, Angelo Calori (have a look at the lintel above the door for his inscribed name), imported marble and tile for the hotel from Italy and the ironwork from England and finished it off with furnishings from New York. It was the height of fashion to have a drink in the bar in the basement and under the street. Light was admitted through glass blocks inlaid into the sidewalk (in fact, many of the merchants who have basement shops in Gastown still have glass blocks set into the sidewalk as part of the lighting for their establishments). Down one side of the hotel is Alexander Street. Alexander is becoming a haven for artists with lofts where artists can live and work, as well as a few art galleries.

Behind the "Gassy Jack" statue is an entrance to an absolutely charming courtyard called **Gaolers Mews** (pronounced "Jailers Mews"). With the wrought-iron fence, the many flowers and trees, and the cobblestones underfoot, it's long been a favorite for film crews. It's also a popular resting spot for people from the surrounding offices to come for a coffee or lunch break. In the back alley, behind the mews, is *Blood Alley*. If you memorize the features of this little cobblestone quarter-block, you'll see it in dozens of TV films and movies. When you exit Gaolers Mews, do so on Carrall Street (where you entered) so you can pop in and visit some of the galleries. Once you reach the end of the block at Cordova Street, turn around and wander back up the other side of Water Street.

DAY ONE: EVENING
Dinner

It's back to Gastown for dinner at the **Raintree at the Landing** (375 Water Street; 604–688–5570; $19 to $28 for entrees). After you've spent the day viewing most of the history the city has to offer, tonight your view will be through one of three large picture windows to the North Shore Mountains, the immense white sails of Canada Place, and probably an Alaska-bound cruise liner loading passengers. Request a window seat, but even those farther back get to see. The exposed beams in the ceiling and the dark red-brick walls with real candles in the wall candleholders make a welcoming environment. The room has a

You Look Familiar

Gastown is a popular filming location. An enormous number of motion pictures and TV shows have been filmed along Alexander Street, in Blood Alley and Gaolers Mews, and on some of the short side streets on the harbor side of Water Street. For Legends of the Fall, *Alexander Street was filled with mud, the buildings were touched up, and horses, wagons, and red-white-and-blue bunting was added. Have a look along Alexander Street when you're standing in front of the "Gassy Jack" statue. Does it look familiar yet? Which scene was it? Other movies and TV shows shot in this small area are* Millennium, X-Files, Viper, Sentinel, Poltergeist, Outer Limits, Sliders, Look Who's Talking, Jumanji, *and* The Commish.

huge fireplace that a person could almost stand in; during warmer weather a vase filled with a colorful array of fresh flowers stands in the opening.

No matter what else you try, we suggest you not miss the excellent Raintree Dungeness Crab Cakes with black bean vinaigrette and summer greens to start. The restaurant emphasizes seafood, but you'll also find meat and chicken choices. Jaded palates can start with the peppered ostrich carpaccio with mountain goat cheese dressing. The servings are liberal and so pleasingly presented that it's almost a pity to dig in.

For a drink and a little music and people-watching, step across the Landing to the **Steamworks Brewing Company** (375 Water Street; 604–689–2739). Because of the lay of the streets, exiting the Raintree indoors into the Landing is only steps from the inside door to the Steamworks. The outside route, back out the front door of the Raintree, is almost a block—you'll have fun figuring that out (or cheat and ask the maitre d'). Coffee drinkers will appreciate the Java and the people-watching at a streetside table at **Starbucks Coffee Co.** (199 Water Street; 604–669–6297). It has a great location, on the corner of Cambie and Water

Streets, about a block downhill on the same side of the street. You'll find a wide range of coffees, steamed milks, and dessert nibbles. If you aren't too stuffed, try an almond-flavored confection called a Copenhagen.

DAY TWO: MORNING
Breakfast

Breakfast at the "O Canada" House is served with crystal and linens at a long table in the dining room or at a smaller table in the second parlor. Sink your teeth into a buttery scone or two, followed by fruit and the main dish of eggs Benedict or salmon crepes. The menu rotates throughout the week, so even if you stay a week, you'll get a different dish each day.

oɕo

After eating your fill, take a right turn out the front door of the "O Canada" House to Burrard Street; then turn left onto Robson Street. At the former library, now Virgin Records and Planet Hollywood, you'll be able to catch a city tour by **The Vancouver Trolley Company** (604–451–5581 or 888–451–5581; departures approximately every thirty minutes between 9:00 A.M. and 6:00 P.M., but it's important to call to check the schedule; operates daily from April to October; one-day ticket is $20). These bright red turn-of-the-century trolleys, with padded wooden seats and big windows, visit many of Vancouver's major attractions. The trip is fully narrated, so you'll learn all about the city as you travel along. The day ticket allows you to stay on for the entire circuit, which takes two hours, or to get on and off at your leisure. The trolley makes sixteen stops at such places as the **Rose Garden,** the **Aquarium,** the **totem poles in Stanley Park,** and the **Dr. Sun Yat-Sen Classical Chinese Garden** in **Chinatown.** It's a simple system: Anytime you want to stop and visit, hop off and look around to your heart's content. When you're ready to leave, reboard another trolley and continue on your way. Your ticket is good until you have done one complete circuit. You'll get a brochure with a timetable on it when you first board the trolley.

DAY TWO: AFTERNOON
Lunch

One of the stops you can make is in **Yaletown,** a character neighborhood full of galleries, shops, and restaurants in renovated warehouses, that has become quite trendy. This up-and-coming area has a wide selection of eateries to choose from. You might wish to make a bit of cash or what have you by challenging your shadow to a game of billiards during your sustenance break. Stop in at the **Yaletown Brewing Co.** (1111 Mainland Street; 604–681–2739), where novices are welcome and an upscale pub and restaurant are frequented by the city's yuppie faction.

❦

Don't worry about your bags after you've checked out of your B&B; you're welcome to leave them at "O Canada" House all day while you continue to tour about. The owners will give you a key to the front door, and you're free to use the parlors, pantry, and main-floor restroom throughout the day.

FOR MORE ROMANCE

There is something romantic about looking back in time and seeing how simple life was (wasn't it?). The **Hastings Mill Museum** (1575 Alma, on the ocean; 604–734–1212; open daily 11:00 A.M. to 4:00 P.M. June to September and weekends only during winter) is housed in the oldest building in Vancouver. The Hastings Mill Store, which survived the great downtown Vancouver fire, was moved many years ago by water from the foot of Main Street to its present location. It has quite a collection of furniture, artifacts, and Indian baskets donated by old Vancouver families who lived in the area during the early days. The museum is privately owned, and admission is by donation. The **Vancouver Museum** (1100 Chestnut; 604–736–4431; open daily 10:00 a.m. to 5:00 P.M.; $5.00 admission) has exhibits on the history of Vancouver, including fashions from the late 1800s and early 1900s.

KUNG HEI FAT CHOY: CHINATOWN

*V*ancouver's Chinatown is the second largest in North America. Large numbers of Chinese came to British Columbia during the late 1800s Gold Rush and during the building of the Canadian Pacific Railway. More recently, thousands of Chinese from Hong Kong sought Canadian passports as a lifeline should the British handover of the colony to the Beijing government go awry. Many of these newcomers have settled in Richmond, a suburb of Vancouver, and created a fusion of upbeat, affluent Asian and North American cultures that looks like any other affluent North American city. But the old Chinatown—ahh, now that is an experience.

If someone were to drop you blindfolded in Chinatown, you'd open your eyes and not believe you were in downtown Vancouver. Chinatown is a visual and sensual delight that is perfect for the heightened senses of lovers. You'll find many experiences to savor with one another. Much of the excitement goes on outside, on the sidewalks: such hustle and bustle, with customers shouting queries and vendors hawking their wares—all vying for limited space. Driving into Chinatown is even more of a culture shock. One moment you're driving in orderly traffic on wide boulevards; then, turning the corner, you find that cars hardly move as trucks double-park to unload vegetables, pedestrians amble across the street everywhere or stop in the middle to have quick conversations, and people spill from the sidewalks. The sounds, smells, signs, buildings, and storefronts are distinctly different from those of the block before. Except for the autos, you could be wandering hand in hand through a Chinese neighborhood of fifty years ago.

Practical notes: Unless you're lucky enough to find on-street parking, put your car in the **CMA Plaza and Parkade** at 180 Keefer (at the corner of Quebec Street), or park well outside Chinatown. Be warned: Moving a car around the area is a slow procedure. The other alternative is even better: Take public transportation.

Romance at a Glance

♥ *Sample the dim sum at the Floata Seafood Restaurant (604–602–0368).*

♥ *Meditate in the Dr. Sun Yat-Sen Classical Chinese Garden (604–689–7133).*

♥ *Hug the Sam Kee Building.*

♥ *Explore Chinatown's every nook.*

♥ *Dine on the exotic at the Phnom Penh Restaurant (604–682–5777).*

MORNING
Brunch

Start your Chinatown visit with a dim sum brunch at the 1,000-seat **Floata Seafood Restaurant** (400–180 Keefer Street; 604–602–0368; dim sum Saturday and Sunday; 8:00 A.M. to 3:00 P.M.; $3.00 to $5.50 per item) in the CMA Plaza and Parkade (the same complex where you left your car). Dim sum is the Chinese equivalent of Spanish tapas, small samples of various steamed or fried dishes, usually a quarter to a fifth of an a la carte order. Normally you would order two to three dishes per person, but start slowly and see how your appetite goes. In the Floata are some English and Chinese signs to help you, or you can resort to the universally understood expedient of pointing. Also the staff does speak English, a fact we mention because it's easy to forget when all you're likely to hear around you is Chinese.

☙

After eating, have a look around at some of the CMA shops in the Plaza. The **Kung Yick Cheong Majong** (105–180 Keefer Street; 604–331–6961) store is worth a visit. It's devoted to the supplies needed for mahjong games, with everything from tables to tiles; you might be tempted to take one home with you. Head out to street level and follow Keefer Street westward to Carrall Street. At Carrall Street turn right until you get to West Pender Street. There on the corner you'll see the **Sam Kee Building** (8 West Pender Street), built in 1913. You'll have to be on your toes for this one or you'll miss it. This is the narrowest commercial building in the world, and it's entered in the *Guinness Book of Records* and *Ripley's Believe It or Not*. Give it a hug—it's almost narrow enough.

Across the street is the **Chinese Cultural Centre** (50 East Pender Street; 604–687–0729). Enter through the four-columned **China Gate,** just up the block; it was used originally during Expo '86 for the China Pavilion. The Cultural Centre was built in 1980 to cultivate Chinese heritage.

Cross the courtyard and enter the tranquillity of the **Dr. Sun Yat-Sen Classical Chinese Garden** (578 Carrall Street; 604–689–7133; open daily all year at 10:00 A.M.; closing times vary; $5.25). The garden is a reproduction of private Ming Dynasty gardens in the city of Suzhou several centuries ago and is the first full-scale classical garden built outside

China. All the materials were shipped from China, including the carvings, contorted ornamental limestone rocks, and hand-fired roof tiles. Even the pebbles are from China. Fifty-two artisans labored a year to construct the complex, using tools and construction techniques of the Ming period (A.D. 1368–1644).

Windows shape your views throughout the courtyard, allowing glimpses of banana, Japanese maple, magnolia, and silk trees; scotch pines; flowering almond; and azaleas. Weeping willows, golden in the sun, reflect perfectly in the still pond. The yin and yang of Taoist philosophy is represented everywhere. Soft and hard textures—black bamboo and mondo grass contrasted with nearby limestone obelisks, for instance, or soft flowing water held within stone channels—as well as the round and square openings found throughout the courtyard, all symbols of nature's balance.

On Friday nights from June to September, you can sip tea and enjoy Chinese music while strolling through the garden filled with handmade lanterns. The garden is a delight at any time of year but holds a special magic within its walls after a snowfall and during the spring reawakening. Late in the day at any season has the added attraction of intricate shadows and soft flaxen light to enthrall you.

From the Garden, move next door to visit the recently completed **Museum and Library Complex** (555 Columbia Street; 604–687–0282; Monday to Friday, 9:00 A.M. to 5:00 P.M.; Tuesday and Sunday, 11:00 A.M. to 5:00 P.M.; $3.00 fee). There are exhibits on the early Chinese pioneers in British Columbia.

Soothed and relaxed, wander back out to the streets. (Before you leave the garden, make sure you have your ticket so you can return to this oasis after a walk through the wilder side of Chinatown.) Don't be afraid to stick your nose into shops as you pass—you never know what riches you'll find: fruits, vegetables, and other foodstuffs to be sure, but also china, fabrics, brass, and a host of other merchandise. Those who enjoy cooking must poke around **Ming Wo** (23 East Pender Street; 604–683–7268), which is filled to the rafters with everything you could want for the kitchen and some things you have never seen.

Don't forget to look up as you wander east along West Pender Street. Many of the buildings along this stretch of West Pender, between Carrall and Main, are from the early 1900s and named for the benevolent society or business that built them. During this racially repressive era, this part of the city was a gathering spot for news from China and the place one came to remit earnings back to faraway family. Buildings were built by those who were from the same region or were loosely related. The recessed balconies on some of the structures are examples of traditional Chinese architecture. Check out the Mah Society of North America building, the Chin Wing Chun Society building (1925), or the Cheng Wing Yeong building (1926) in the 200 block of Pender. The oldest buildings in the area date from the late 1880s just after the great Vancouver fire that devastated the old, primarily wooden downtown. The whole area was almost razed several times over the years for redevelopment or freeways but made its final escape from the wrecking ball when Chinatown was designated a provincial historic area in 1971.

Continue along Pender to Gore Street, and turn right for a block. Head down Keefer to Carrall Street. This puts you right back at the garden, where, if you still have your ticket, you can spend a few more quiet moments resting in the serenity there.

EVENING
Dinner

The **Phnom Penh Restaurant** (244 East Georgia Street; 604–682–5777, open 10:00 A.M. to 9:00 P.M.; $5 to $20 for entrees) has won numerous local awards for its Asian food over the years but is still a bit of a secret in town. Francois Huynh, one of the family of owners, left the war in Cambodia for Vietnam and eventually landed in Canada in 1979, penniless. Now on the way to holding a small restaurant empire, the family serves authentic Vietnamese and Cambodian cuisine in an unpretentious atmosphere where you will probably still be served by one of the owners.

The staff will help you order, but we have some definite favorites you won't want to miss. Start with one of the hot and sour soups like Canh Chua Tom (hot and sour soup with prawns) for they are some of the best to be found in all the dozens of Asian restaurants in Vancouver ($9.75; enough for two). Also order the marinated butter beef, thinly sliced rare to very, very rare marinated beef on a bed of brown garlic and cilantro ($8.95). Deep-fried squid or prawns, the grandmother's recipe, may not be recommended by the Heart Association, but the lemon pepper sauce that comes with it is worth the risk ($12.50). For the less exotic but still flavorful, the deep fried spring rolls, barbecued beef brochette, and prawn supreme on sugar cane (OK, so a little exotic) are more familiar tastes. If you find things too bland, add the fish sauce that accompanies the meal to give it a fuller-bodied flavor. Don't leave without sampling a Vietnamese coffee, hot or over ice, and, if you have room, the white bean pudding with coconut milk. Both are unusual takes on familiar themes.

FOR MORE ROMANCE

Visit Chinatown between late May and late September and you can attend the **Night Market** (200 block of Pender Street and Keefer Street). The open-air bazaar, operating on Friday, Saturday, and Sunday nights between 6:30 and 11:30 P.M., is fashioned after night markets in Asia. Try a snack. If you tend to be conservative about what you eat, there's a solution. Just don't ask what it is until after you've had a bite.

ITINERARY 15
Two days and one night

INDIAN SUMMER ON SPANISH BANKS

*L*overs have watched the sun go down from the edge of the cliff behind the Museum of Anthropology for a thousand years. We did as new lovers. It doesn't take much imagination to experience the same thing sweethearts did when First Nations People were the sole inhabitants of the coast. The sunset is just as glorious, and if you squint, the small boats cruising in the distance are orcas basking in the current. To your left the longhouse and totem poles of the museum's exhibit are as resplendent as any chief could have afforded centuries ago. With little effort you can imagine that the two of you are village children. This is your land. The sea breeze brings a hint of kelp and sea salt and the distant traffic is the resonance of the vibrant village life behind you.

The daydream is so easy that it's a shock to turn away from the sea and discover the glass and concrete of the Museum of Anthropology. Now all you can do is go and see your village's accoutrements encased in glass. Labeled and categorized, the everyday is now the extraordinary.

Practical notes: Even though you'll be visiting several beaches, this itinerary is a year-round treat. With the exception of Wreck Beach, all the beaches retain some of their summer flavor even in winter. This itinerary packs in a lot, but all the spots are close to one another. In addition, in midsummer the sun doesn't set until well after 9:00 P.M.

DAY ONE: AFTERNOON

Check in at the **Ogden Point Bed and Breakfast** (1982 Ogden on Kits Point; 604–736–4336; $80 to $180) and drop your bags.

If you love the 1920s and 1930s, you'll find this place a thrill. Recently, the original owner of the house dropped by to meet the new owners, Shirley and Darryle Wheatcroft, and over the course of several months sold them some of the furniture originally used in the house. The grandfather clock now graces the hallway, along with the framed receipt for $95; crating and delivery were an extra $1.00. Shirley and Darryle have lived in the house since the 1960s and have kept the dark paneling and polished fir floors. With the addition of the original furniture, together with the 1920s photographs of the log road in front of the house with beachgoers parking in the brush, you'll swear you're back seventy years.

We think the front room (Room 1) is the best of the three rooms, because it's bigger, looks out on the beach and parkland across the street, and has a terrific nighttime view of the city.

Back to the present, though, there's a lot to see. First head out to the **University of British Columbia.** The drive along the beaches is gorgeous but can be slow in summertime, when half the city lives along the shore during the day. The major interior routes are faster but less colorful.

The **Museum of Anthropology** (6393 Northwest Marine Drive, on the campus of the University of British Columbia; 604–822–3825; open Tuesday through Sunday 11:00 A.M. to 5:00 P.M. and until 9:00 P.M. Tuesday; $6.00 for adults and $3.50 for seniors; 5:00 to 9:00 P.M. on Tuesday evenings, admission is

Romance at a Glance

♥ *Stay at the Ogden Point Bed and Breakfast (604–736–4336).*

♥ *Discover the region's heritage at the Museum of Anthropology (604–822–3825).*

♥ *Contemplate your lover's navel at a Japanese garden (604–822–6038).*

♥ *Wade out along Spanish Banks.*

♥ *Sup at the Brock House Conservatory Restaurant (604–224–3317).*

The entire Nitobe Memorial Garden is an allegory of life. The bridge in the center leads to the Marriage House and is built of seventy-seven logs. Legend has it that only on the seventh day of the seventh month could lovers meet on the bridge of the Celestial Way. You and your lover can decide to take the bridge to marriage or use another path. Upon further exploration you will come to a bench at a dead end that is surrounded by gnarly old bushes and stagnant water. Sitting here on a bench made for two with your lover reminds you that, if you're lucky in love, there is still togetherness to see you through at the end.

free) has one of the best collections of Coast Salish, Gitksan, Haida, Kwakwaka'wakw, Nisga'a, and other Northwest Coast First Nation art in the world. Totem and mortuary poles rescued from the forest are perched on the cliff behind the museum, their wonderful carved faces looking out to sea from both inside the protective cocoon of the museum and on the grounds outdoors. The renowned collection of everyday goods used by the Coast people will draw you into life as it was hundreds of years ago.

Across the road from the museum is the quiet oasis of the **Nitobe Memorial Garden** (604–822–6038; open 10:00 A.M. to 2:30 P.M. weekdays during winter and 10:00 A.M. to 6:00 P.M. during summer; $2.50 entrance fee). Built to honor Dr. Inazo Nitobe, a prominent Japanese statesman of the 1920s and 1930s and a proponent of peace between Japan and the West, the garden has evolved into a lush formal Japanese garden complete with Japanese lanterns and fast-flowing waterfalls.

You must take time to escape across the zigzagging bridge to elude any evil spirits that may be following you. Evil spirits can only travel in straight lines and cannot cross the zigzagging bridge.

Before leaving the peninsula, if you're feeling a little daring, you might try something different that happens in no other major city in North America. During summer thousands of sun worshipers descend the steep trails to the beach at the foot of the cliffs surrounding the Japanese garden and the Museum of Anthropology. At the bottom is **Wreck Beach** (at the end of the peninsula at the University of British Columbia), the city's nude beach. On a sunny day 5,000 people of all ages and stages of undress—from students and professors to the business elite—spend the day sampling tasty Samozas and beer, trying on handmade scarves and jewelry, paddling about in the ocean, and taking in the view of the Gulf Islands. Enterprising shopkeepers haul propane tanks, umbrellas, coolers, and barbecues down the path for a full day of fixing up culinary delights. (At the end of a long day, hauling all that gear up the steep path to the road is a Herculean feat.)

The city has always been divided between the more liberal European influence concerning dress for the beach and the straight-and-narrow interpretation of what constitutes moral decay. Periodically, overdressed guardians of the moral fiber of the nation's youth descend the cliffs en masse to march the beach with condemning placards. Of course, the beach crowd loves a parade and join in sans clothes. Others, too sun-lazy to move, applaud the theater from their logs. The entrepreneurs see the mass demonstrators as just more customers and try to sell them everything from tuna fish sandwiches to sandals. Whether or not you dress for the beach Wreck Beach's avant-garde, counterculture party atmosphere is guaranteed to loosen your inhibitions and bring out your rebellious streak.

If you and your partner spent too much time and money selecting your togs to just drop them unseen in the sand, you might prefer another of the city's premier beaches, **Spanish Banks.** Named for the Spanish doubloon lost by one of the first Spanish explorers and found many years ago in the sand, the beach affords a spectacular view of the city, the North Shore Mountains, and the islands.

Each beach in the city has its own character and flavor, and Spanish Banks, with its wide paths and unobstructed views, was made especially for a lovers' stroll. At low tide the two of you can kick off your shoes and walk out to the middle of the bay perhaps 0.5 mile on the hard-packed sand. Tidal pools warmed in the sun for hours are a perfect place to wade a bit. When the tide turns, it comes in so slowly that you'll have plenty of time to walk back in to shore.

To get to Spanish Banks from the Nitobe Memorial Garden or Wreck Beach, drive along Northwest Marine Drive back toward the city. The curvy road down the hill from the University of British Columbia to the beaches is only a few blocks long, and some of the city's ritzy houses line the residential area on your right. (Note that 2 blocks east from the Nitobe Memorial Garden, Northwest Marine Drive turns off toward the left along the sea. The divided road straight ahead is the wrong direction.) Park at the first parking lot at the bottom of the hill, so that no matter how far you walk, you'll always have the hill as a landmark to guide you directly back to your car. When you're ready for dinner, head back to Ogden Point Bed and Breakfast to dress.

DAY ONE: EVENING
Dinner

To get to the Brock House, simply go back out to the main road, Cornwall, and turn right. Keep the sea to your right and continue as Cornwall turns into Point Grey Road. Don't worry about going too far; you'll end up in a cul-de-sac at a park, and the circular driveway of the **Brock House Conservatory Restaurant** (3875 Point Grey Road; 604–224–3317; $19 to $29) is just a block back. Dress is West Coast formal, meaning casually elegant—only baseball caps, jeans, and sneakers are frowned upon.

The palatial 1912 residence-turned-restaurant is set on two and a half acres of prime waterfront property with 300 feet of sandy beach. Noted architect Samuel Maclure designed a twenty-room, nine-fireplace showpiece that, as the home of the Brock family, hosted guests from around the world. Reginald Brock, dean of the University of British Columbia for a number of years, used the building as a hospitality house for his many guests. After he and his wife were killed in a plane crash, the house ended up in the hands of the city of Vancouver, which now leases it to the Brock House Society. The house at present serves as an activity center for seniors and a restaurant in the evenings and on weekends, as well as being a favorite location for weddings and fashion shows.

To savor your feast, definitely sit in the graceful, glass-enclosed conservatory, with its spectacular view of the city, sea, and mountains. The Caesar salad for two, prepared at your table, is top-notch. Although you'll find several tasty meat and pasta dishes, seafood fans should stick with the fresh fish, scallops, prawns, or oysters. Most dishes are prepared with a scrumptious sauce, but purists can ask for the sauce on the side. As connoisseurs of pecan pie—we once did a pecan pie tour of Georgia, home of the pecan pie—we can highly recommend the Bourbon Street Pecan Pie. Although Pecan Pie Light is an oxymoron, there is such a thing, and it's just as delicious but has 50 percent less calories: Just ask the waiter to split one piece for the two of you.

❧

If the day's walking and the sumptuous dinner don't lull you to sleep, take in some of the live music at one of the little cafes on Cornwall Street just up the street from your B&B.

Day Two: Morning

Kitsilano Beach, also fondly referred to as Kits Beach, hops from early in the morning until late at night, especially in summer. Make a point of rising before 8:00 A.M. and walking along the quiet beach to the pool at the far end (about 6 blocks) for an early-morning swim. The still, azure water of **Kits Pool** (open spring to late summer only) with the backdrop of the mountains reflecting a hint of gold from the morning sun is about as good as life gets. A languorous swim with your lover is a playful way to work up an appetite.

Breakfast

Here's another reason to choose Room 1 at the Ogden Point: Your breakfast of straight-from-the-oven croissants with yummy homemade jams and jellies, fresh seasonal fruit, just-squeezed orange juice, and tea and coffee is served on your own private veranda.

❖

Call in at the **Maritime Museum** (1905 Ogden; 604–257–8300; open 10:00 A.M. to 5:00 P.M. Tuesday to Sunday; $6.00 for adults) directly across the street from the Ogden Point Bed and Breakfast. In addition to the hundreds of old photos and the displays of famous ships that have plied the British Columbia coast, the museum houses the *St. Roch,* an RCMP ketch that patrolled the West Coast of Canada and the Arctic for many years. Don't miss the piers just behind the museum, where special visiting boats are often docked. You're as likely to find an old fire boat or a Chinese junk as you are a lovingly restored, 1930s classic cabin cruiser with richly polished teak decks.

DAY TWO: AFTERNOON

Kits Beach is one of the places to be seen if you're young and active. On a sunny weekend in summer, there are probably more musclemen and string-bikini-clad women per square yard here than any other place in the province. Volleyball is played in earnest, and serves on the tennis courts behind the beach have been known to rip through the chain-link fence. Whereas it would be bad form to draw attention to your body on Wreck Beach, Kits Beach is the place to show off with as little on as the city bylaws allow.

Musicians, hot dog stands, Rollerblades, bikes, kite flying, dogs, children, smelt fishermen, barbecuers, sailboats, lovers, and an occasional eagle make for an entertaining afternoon of people-watching. Several choices for sit-down meals are at the entrance to the beach on Cornwall Avenue, but if it's sunny, our preference is to grab a snack from the snack bar and cuddle on one of the benches or in the sand. The beach show is some of the best entertainment in town and is guaranteed to make you smile.

For More Romance

After dinner at the Brock House, walk hand in hand along the oceanfront path in **Jericho Park,** a block to your right as you exit the restaurant. The sunset reflected in the windows of the downtown skyscrapers turns the city to a dazzling gold, and the beach sand will warm your bodies long after the sun has disappeared.

ITINERARY 16
One day

TREASURE HUNTING

"One person's rubbish is another person's treasure." Few would argue the point, and a fast look around a friend's house will confirm it. For some, treasures are found only in antiques stores of repute; for others, a flea market is the place to search out hidden goodies. Rare books, comic books, costume jewelry, gems, silver, and gold are all treasures to someone. And much of the pleasure of the treasure is in the hunt. . . . As you stroll among the junk and the jewels, see if you can't find something your loved one would consider a gem to fondle, exclaim over, perchance to buy.

Practical notes: You'll have to make a decision based on your interests. If you die for flea markets, you'll need to do this itinerary over the weekend, as the Vancouver Flea Market is open only on Saturday and Sunday. The city holds hundreds of antiques and collectibles stores, and the itinerary we've selected keeps traveling to a minimum. Still, you'll be happier doing this in a car, although the downtown stores can easily be done on foot.

MORNING

Breakfast

There are lots of opportunities to munch along the route today, but for those of you who like to start by grazing, stop by **Ecco il Pane** (2563 West Broadway; 604–739–1314; $7 to $9). The French toast is delicious, the atmosphere noisy and upbeat, and the coffee will give you that edge you'll need later when you are negotiating for some fabulous prize.

ᘛᘚ

The Vancouver Flea Market (703 Terminal Avenue; 604–685–0666; open Saturday, Sunday, and holidays 9:00 A.M. to 5:00 P.M.) is a good place to start on Saturday morning. You can enter for the princely sum of 60 cents. There are two schools of thought about when to go: Either arrive there early for the best choice or pull in just before closing on Sunday and get the best deals as vendors try to unload leftovers. Aficionados go early Saturday morning when treasures haven't been scooped. If you see an item that's just a bit too pricey, it might be worth a return visit late Sunday, when prices are at their best. Bargaining is always apropos. The Vancouver Flea Market is definitely a "treasures and trash" kind of place. The flea market is housed in a huge great red barn of a building. More than 350 tables are laid out inside with a range of goods that will astound you—from boat motors and the latest in cowboy paraphernalia to computers and bric-a-brac. On sunny day additional tables spill out the door onto the parking lot and sidewalks out front.

Romance at a Glance

♥ *Search the city for treasures.*

♥ *Watch the sun go down as you take a Sunset Dinner Cruise (604–688–8072).*

♥ *Have an after-cruise drink at Bridges Pub (604–687–4400).*

♥ *Listen to jazz at the Cotton Club (604–738–7465).*

AFTERNOON

Lunch

Stop for lunch before continuing on your quest. **Athene's Restaurant** (3618 West Broadway; 604–731–4135; open 11:30 A.M. to 11:30 P.M.; luncheon entrees $8 to $11) is within a couple of blocks of your next stop. You'll find the food flavorful and the atmosphere loud and boisterous. Greek food is made for sharing tidbits, and as a shopping tactic both of you should have a bit of garlic-laden tzatziki. This will help immensely to put a little pressure on shopkeepers when you're negotiating.

⊙†⊙

For the afternoon foray start at **Folkart Interiors** (3651 West Tenth Avenue; 604–731–7576; open 10:00 A.M. to 6:00 P.M., Sunday 12:00 to 5:00 P.M.), for Canadiana furnishings, cedar wood carvings by local artists, reproductions and real farmhouse antiques, and other crafts. Across the street is **Angela James Ltd.** (3720 West Tenth Avenue; 604–224–8664; open 10:00 A.M. to 6:00 P.M., Sunday 12:00 to 5:00 P.M.), which carries pine and Old English–style reproductions and some antiques. For the real thing drive up to the shopping area of West Tenth Avenue. There you'll find **Canada West Antiques** (4430 West Tenth Avenue; 604–222–9190; open 10:30 A.M. to 5:30 P.M.), which specializes in antique pine furniture, French Provincial, and treasures imported from "La Belle Province" of Quebec.

Back down Fourth Avenue the **Comicshop** (2089 West Fourth Avenue; 604–738–8122; open daily 10:00 A.M. to 6:00 P.M.) has a wide array of comic books, with both new and collector editions. The shop has been around for more than twenty-three years, long enough for some of its original purchases to become collectible. If more highbrow books speak to you, go to **Albion Books** (523 Richard Street, at the corner of Pender Street; 604–662–3113; open daily 10:00 A.M. to 5:30 P.M.), which has a wealth of secondhand books and even a small selection of first editions and collectibles. **Antiquarius** (207 West Hastings, Suite 609; 604–669–7288; open 11:00 A.M. to 5:00 P.M. Monday to Saturday) has a bounty of paper ephemera, including old posters, magazines, letters, signed portraits, postcards, autographs, photographs, tourist brochures, menus, old legal documents, and tickets. Nearby **McLeod's Books** (455 West Pender Street, corner of Pender Street; 604–681–7654; open 10:00 A.M. to 5:30 P.M. Monday to Saturday) is piled high with books of all sorts, many of them used or out of print. McLeod's also has a selection of autographs and manuscripts primarily from Western Canadians but some from famous people everyone would recognize. As you walk toward the waterfront, **Cabbages and Kinx** (315 West Hastings; 604–669–4238) has an eclectic mix of vintage clothing and funky cosmetics, and **Deluxe Junk** (310 West Cordova Street; 604–685–4871) carries vintage clothing and accessories.

A couple of blocks away is the **Three Centuries Shop** (321 Water Street; 604–685–8808), specializing in nineteenth-century European antiques, while the **Inuit Gallery,** almost next door (345 Water Street; 604–688–7323; open 10:00 A.M. to 6:00 P.M. Monday to Saturday and noon to 5:00 P.M. Sunday) has newer creations of Native art. Around the corner on Cordova is another antiques store of note, **Bona-Wight Antiques and Collectibles** (72 Cordova Street; 604–608–1986), and it warrants more than a few minutes. Even if you have to travel a distance, one of those handmade carpets hanging high up on the wall could be rolled up neatly without too much trouble.

EVENING

Dinner

As the original treasure hunters were also often sailors of the high seas, a cruise is on the menu for this evening. **Champagne Cruises** (100–1676 Duranleau; 604–688–8072; year-round; $49.95 plus tax or $25.00 for just the cruise) has a Sunset Dinner Cruise departing every night at 5:30 P.M. and returning about 8:00 P.M. The yacht's layout boasts picture windows for viewing the sights of Vancouver Harbour, English Bay, the mouth of the Capilano River, Lions Gate Bridge, Spanish Banks, Stanley Park, millionaire estates, and

Big Ring Box

Most auction houses auction off unopened boxes of belongings from commercial public storage warehouses when the owners don't claim their property or pay the rent for a long time. Grownups act like children at Christmas, claiming their prize and tearing open the containers right on the auction floor, dumping the contents everywhere. And no wonder. One bidder claimed a small box for $10 and opened it to find an expensive ring, a strand of pearls, and other jewelry—enough for several anniversary gifts. Complete silver sets, china for eight, crystal, handmade quilts, expensive and exotic knickknacks, fur coats, and violins have all emerged from deep storage.

University of British Columbia properties. You'll feast on such tasties as barbecued British Columbia salmon or marinated chicken filets, with salads and vegetables, but the highlight of the cruise is leaning on the rail hand in hand and watching the sun go down behind the mountains and the city lights come up.

৹৵৹

Don't head home too early. For a nightcap stop in at **Bridges Pub** (1696 Duranleau Street, Granville Island; 604–687–4400), the big yellow building right beside the disembarkation point from your dinner cruise. And for live jazz meander over to the **Cotton Club** (200–1833 Anderson, Granville Island; 604–738–7465; 11:00 to 1:00 A.M.), a couple of blocks away near the entrance to the island.

FOR MORE ROMANCE

If you arrive in Vancouver midweek, take advantage of the auctions, where prices can be exceedingly low. **Tyldesley's** (1339 Kingsway; 604–874–4238; open Monday to Friday from

9:00 A.M. to 5:00 P.M.) has auctions on Tuesday at noon and 7:00 P.M., and you can preview the merchandise on Monday afternoons. **Love's** (1635 West Broadway; 604–733–1157) has viewing on Tuesday and Wednesday (call for precise times) and holds auctions on Wednesday at midday and 7:00 P.M. **Maynard's Auctioneers** (415 West Second Avenue; 604–876–6787; open 9:00 A.M. to 5:00 P.M.) has auctions for home furnishings most Wednesdays, and art and antique auctions are held on occasion. Phone for times.

RIGHT PLACE, RIGHT TIME

ITINERARY 17
Two days and one night

POPPING THE QUESTION

*H*aving trouble popping the big question? Every time you think about asking for that lifetime commitment, a leopard grabs your tongue and albatrosses flap through your stomach. You know your love will say yes, but what if the person doesn't? Take a page from savvy politicians and run the idea out for a little prescreening to see how receptive your spouse-to-be is to the idea. Nothing as overt as a straight question, just not-so-subtle hints.

Practical notes: You're going to an Italian wedding, so pull out your finery. Get gussied up, if you want; this is no time to be shy. Your little-worn tux or that smart little well-out-of-date hat with the veil and beads will actually fit in just fine. It's imperative that your spouse-to-be have an agreeable early-morning disposition. Otherwise, skip the balloon trip and sleep in, have the brunch at the Café Pacifica in the Pan Pacific Hotel, and bask in the pool with a view. For the balloon flight dress in layers. The balloon tends to be much warmer than the surrounding air, and the temperature rises as the day comes alive. Take your camera!

DAY ONE: AFTERNOON

Romance at a Glance

♥ *Dance on the tables at La Ventana, a delicious little Spanish restaurant (604–682–8667).*

♥ *Check into the Pan Pacific Hotel (604–662–8111).*

♥ *Linger at La Senza Lingerie in Pacific Centre (604–685–2380).*

♥ *Visit Birks Jewelers to inspect fine jewelry and rings (604–669–3333).*

♥ *Take in Tony n' Tina's Wedding (604–280–3311).*

♥ *Smell the flowers at the Four Seasons Hotel's Garden Terrace for a night cap (604–689–9333).*

♥ *Pop the question at 2,000 feet in a hot air balloon (604–533–2701).*

Lunch

Start your campaign by letting your partner know what a happy-go-lucky kind of person you are. Take your mate to a little upbeat Spanish restaurant where, if you feel frisky, the proprietors will let you dance around with a rose in your teeth. You'll need the sustenance and the positive atmosphere for what's to come.

La Ventana (162 Water Street, in Gastown; 604–682–8667; tapas, $6.50 to $8.50; entrees, $13.00 to $21.00), run by experienced restaurateur Fernando Garcia, has a few things going for it. First, the food is fabulous. Make a meal from the tapas and share each dish with your lover. Succulent pimientos de piquillo, red peppers stuffed with seafood and topped with lobster sauce, or dainty *croquetas,* deep-fried with a creamy center and served with aioli, are excellent choices. But order two of the *cazuela de setas* to avoid a fight. The broth that the assorted mushrooms are sautéed in with garlic, shallots, and olive oil has caused a rift for more than one couple as each eyed the last morsel. Still hungry? The *pa amb tomaquet*—garlic bread with tomato and herb olive oil and cured ham and cheese, a Catalonian favorite—will fill any leftover space you may have. The restaurant is in one of the older buildings in Gastown, and the huge fir beams, the exposed brick, the brass and glass accents, and the colorful artwork give the place an upscale feel. Moreover, the staff are friendly and very Spanish—it won't take much to get them to break out the castanets.

〇✼〇

Later check into the **Pan Pacific Hotel** (300–999 Canada Place; 604–662–8111), home-away-from-home for princes and princesses, presidents, ministers, and all manner of romantic couples looking for the ultimate view of the harbor from the bedroom or bath. The Pan Pacific has one of the most spectacular views overlooking the harbor and the North Shore Mountains of any place in Vancouver. If you're on a budget, opt for one of the deluxe Harbor View Rooms ending in 10 above the fifteenth floor. (Note that we did not say how big a budget; prices can range from $209 to $430, depending on the season and promotions.) These are the corner suites facing the water and have the most expansive views of downtown, Stanley Park, Lions Gate Bridge, and some of the mountains. To really compress your wallet, reserve a Mountain Suite on the north side of the hotel ($420 to $700) or ask for the Royal Suite, named after Prince Charles and Princess Diana stayed in the room in 1986.

At $2,000 a day skip the rest of this itinerary, because we're sure your partner will be certain you are serious about him or her moments after walking in the door. (Normally frugal couples should avoid springing this surprise on their mate without smelling salts.) Besides, there's enough to do in the room without venturing outside. We'd be the first to invite friends to drop by to help run up the room-service bill and bathe in the Jacuzzi with a view. The place is large enough to have a rousing game of hide-and-seek after you kick them out.

Plebeians will have to content themselves with a swim in the heated outdoor pool on the eighth floor. This is especially invigorating in late December. Swimming during a snowfall is a thrill most people never get to enjoy. Failing a snow shower, enjoy the view while you tread water.

By now your partner should have a severely arched eyebrow. To keep your love in suspense about your intentions, you might spend the rest of afternoon doing a little window shopping at one of the larger malls in Vancouver, just up the street from the hotel. Start at **La Senza Lingerie** (Pacific Centre at Georgia and Howe, on the second floor about halfway down the mall; 604–685–2380) by perusing the lingerie. Depending on how daring you feel,

you might inveigle your spouse-to-be to try on something a little revealing. The guys look especially good in the satin PJs, but the staff gets nervous. When you leave the lingerie store (or are asked to leave), hop across the mall to **Holt Renfrew** (Pacific Centre—take a right and it's just a few doors down; 604–681–3121), a chi chi upscale clothier with magnificent furs that, assuming you're not in full-camouflage hunting regalia, the staff will let you try on. Fur, real or faux, has a certain sensuality associated with its softness, but try to keep the petting to a minimum. Also in Holt Renfrew are those clothes you'd love to be caught dead in (or any other way) that sell in the middle five figures and up. For those prices you should have Mr. G. Armani personally waiting on you. Fortunately, window shopping is free.

Now it's entirely possible that by this time your consort has completely misconstrued your message and the rest of this itinerary is moot since the two of you won't see the light of day until next week. But if you're still with us, sashay down to **Birks Jewelers** to make the message clearer. (Henry Birks and Sons Inc., to be precise, which you should be if you are going to shop there; 698 West Hastings Street, about 2 blocks back toward the hotel;

604–669–3333). You can go outside to reach the store, but it's more fun to window-shop through the rest of the Pacific Centre across Dunsmuir Street on the shopping overpass and into the Atrium before exiting on the Granville Street side. Birks is one of the city's oldest and most reputable jewelers and has the ambience to match. When you window-shop for a ring here, your soon-to-be-spouse will know you have discerning taste and elegance despite your dime-store tennis shoes. In fact, to impress him or her with your impeccable sense of style, "discover" the estate-jewelry counter just inside the Hasting Street entrance, the first counter to your left. Some of these pieces are outdated cuts or settings, but others are extraordinary for their unique designs that speak eloquently of one person's love for another in days gone by.

Skipping over to Howe Street, window-shop your way back up toward Robson Street (back inside the Pacific Centre if it's raining). Of course, you'll need an outfit to take away on your honeymoon, so start by shopping for the proper cruise attire (you will make an appearance on deck at some point, won't you?). If he insists you have one of those invisible string bikinis that cost $100, march him immediately down to the **Just Cruisin' Shoppe** (890 Howe Street; 604–688–2030). If he will, you will, so hand him the men's version (perversion?) of the matching his-and-hers bikini briefs. If he calls your buff and agrees to show you his, make him go first and then wait near the busy front window while he changes.

Don't shop 'till you drop because there is a long night ahead. Retrace your steps to the hotel and have a languorous predinner swim or head over to the **Gerald Lounge** at the Sutton Place Hotel (845 Burrard; 604–682–5511) for a predinner drink. Celebrities have been known to lurk in the shadows here so don't be surprised if you come face to face with a TV or movie idol.

DAY ONE: EVENING

You have a standing invitation to **Tony n' Tina's Wedding** (tickets at 604–280–3311; $60 to $65), and they'll set a date as soon as you call to let them know you're coming. Tony n'

Tina's Wedding is a live comedy where you can't tell the actors from the paying guests. You'll be mingling with other members of the audience and the cast throughout the performance, and this is your chance to let your wackier self go. Be creative: If you have a secret desire to be someone else—a countess, movie star, or a dentist from Des Moines—play it tonight. Who's to know or care?

The evening starts with your arrival at **St. Andrew's Wesley Church** (corner of Burrard and Nelson Streets) for the ceremony of marriage between Tina Vitale and Tony Nunzio. The doors to the church open at 6:00 P.M., and the ceremony starts at 6:30 P.M. Don't be late; arrive right at 6:00 so you don't miss meeting the feuding families and the bride and groom's friends. As you sit in the pews, those around you may or may not be actors. Even more intriguing, they don't know if you're an actor either, so if you feel adventurous, you can collect kisses from complete strangers you take a fancy to ("Dahling, so goood to see you again." Right cheek, left cheek) or you can introduce your partner to others as "Tony's cousin, the tarantula trainer from Atlanta."

After the ceremony you'll move from the church to **Chardonnay's Restaurant** (corner of Hastings and Howe Streets) for the wedding reception. You could find yourself seated at one of the big long tables with strangers—just as you would be at a regular wedding. While you eat—choose the salmon if it's offered; the waiter assured us it's the best of the typical wedding-reception fare (no choice for dessert; wedding cake only)—you'll be hilariously entertained by the events continuing on around you. For the main theme there's the not-quite-Vegas-style act, with the restaurant owner/father of the bride as the master of ceremonies, but little vignettes are happening all over the room constantly throughout the evening. Don't expect real life, even in the restrooms—you're likely to find the play going on there too. Anything can happen. You may find yourselves drawn into a raging lovers' quarrel on one side or the other or crushed in a booth between two oblivious and passionate lovers.

No matter how shy you are when you start out, before long you'll find yourselves singing and dancing with the rest of the crowd. At the end of the evening, even with a playbill, you still won't know if the couple behind you were actors or guests. Tony n' Tina's Wedding plays on Wednesday through Saturday nights year-round and also on Tuesday nights from June through August.

After the wedding you'll want to gossip a bit about your friends Tony and Tina, so head over to the **Garden Terrace** in the Four Seasons Hotel (791 West Georgia; 604–689–9333) for a nightcap before bed. The Four Seasons is about 1½ blocks away on Howe, and the lounge is up the escalators past the front desk. (You can't miss the floral bouquet that greets you at the top of the escalator. The stargazer lilies do need to be appreciated to flourish, so make the appropriate noises when you sniff their heavenly fragrance.) Seats are far enough apart that you have a little privacy, and the plants and shrubs surrounding you make it intimate.

DAY TWO: MORNING
Breakfast

It's entirely possible that your mate will think you're full of hot air when you tell him or her what time you have to be at the launch site for your balloon excursion with **Pegasus Ballooning** (24202 56 Avenue, Langley; 604–533–2701; flights are weather-dependent; $350 per couple; weddings can be arranged). Room service is the order of the day, and you can eat in between showering and dressing. The early-morning hour is to ensure smooth sailing, so the pilot says, when you pop the question. (In your favor is that most people can be counted on to be docile before 6:00 A.M.) At any rate, watching the sun rising on a new era as you coast noiselessly over the countryside seems only fitting for this momentous occasion. Slipping slowly through the still morning, you can hear even a whispered conversation on the ground as you float by. (Balloons coast at the speed of the wind, so there's no breeze at all. Most people do not have a sensation of flying, because the craft moves so slowly.) A gentle "Hello" is the appropriate way to announce your presence to the unfortunates on the ground who feel something stealing over them but don't know from where. Dogs howl, horses neigh, and babies cry as the 8-story structure glides just above the treetops overhead at a stately 4 or 5 miles an hour. The flight begins in the Fraser Valley, which has some of the most dramatic scenery in North America, including the Coast Mountains and the high snowcovered volcano Mount Baker.

We suggest that sometime during the sixty- to ninety-minute flight you make your move. If there is any suggestion that you may be "dumped," do it near the end of the trip, when you are closer to the ground. The pilot, David Gleed, has had lots of experience and can be counted on to help let you down gently should the worst happen.

FOR MORE ROMANCE

For a personally conducted tour of Vancouver in a restored Ford Model A Phaeton Touring Car, try **Fridge's Early Motion Tours Ltd.** (1–1380 Thurlow Street; 604–687–5088; $80 per hour; reserve ahead for a time, at any time of year). Fridge will take you to the shopping hot spot of Robson Street, through Stanley Park, to English Bay, Chinatown, and Gastown. You and your mate are guaranteed to be the center of attention in this one-of-a-kind car, so smile brightly. A Polaroid picture of you and the car is included in the price.

ITINERARY 18
One day

CAROL SHIPS

*I*n darkest December the city wears its finest jewels to celebrate the lengthening days after the winter solstice. It's time for the two of you to ignore the chill, gather up your gloves and scarves, and venture out. Necklaces of rubies, sapphires, diamonds, and emeralds adorn the skyscrapers, and the working cranes of the city compete to have the most colorful superstructure. Brightly colored presents smothered in ribbons and bows beckon from shop windows, and there really are chestnuts roasting on an open fire at the street corner. Carolers, singing both offkey and on, warble their joy to the grinning crowds of onlookers. It's the spirit that counts, isn't it? The city's restaurants and hotels are dripping with tinsel—good places for a mug of cheer. So get out and enjoy the wonder.

Practical notes: This itinerary takes place during December, so dress warmly. Check the exact dates of the Carol ships and VanDusen Botanical Garden light display. Starting times for various events do change so be sure to call and confirm.

AFTERNOON

Romance at a Glance

♥ *Enjoy lunch at the Century Grill (604–688–8088).*

♥ *Explore the delightful wares at Chintz and Company (604–689–2022).*

♥ *Wonder at the holiday displays at The Sutton Place Hotel (604–682–5511), Four Seasons Hotel (604–689–9333), and Canada Place (604–666–8477).*

♥ *Meander through the Festival of Lights at VanDusen Botanical Garden (604–257–8666).*

♥ *Sing your heart out on an excursion with Vancouver Champagne Cruises Inc. (604–688–8072).*

Lunch

Start with lunch at the **Century Grill** (1095 Hamilton Street; 604–688–8088; $6 to $13), a grill and oyster bar in the converted warehouse district of Yaletown. It has a warm, appealing atmosphere, with deep red-and-rust brick walls and enormous exposed beams. Spotlights glinting off the glassware and bottles in the bar area add a twinkle here and there, complementing the dark honey-colored leather on the seating and the pristine white tablecloths.

The chef makes a particularly tasty fresh roasted turkey club sandwich, a colorful dish with cranberry sauce and avocado that is immense enough to be shared. Ask to have it cut in four pieces or munching with decorum will be a challenge. On a cold day the chicken soup is also a good body-warmer: as the Century Grill menu says, "So good you'll want to pinch our cheeks." Finish off with the banana cream pie, prepared with toasted almonds and whipped cream.

❦

Walk up the block to explore the home-furnishing temptations at **Chintz and Company** (950 Homer Street; 604–689–2022). Featured here are two floors loaded with everything to decorate your home—urns, wooden and silk flowers, cushions, pillows, linens, bedding, dishes, glassware, paper goods, sofas, chairs, tables, upholstery fabrics, tassels, ribbons, and trims of every description—all imported from craft havens worldwide.

Tour up Smithe Street to Burrard Street to **The Sutton Place Hotel** (845 Burrard Street; 604–682–5511) for the first magical display of holiday trees decorated by the airline and cruise-line industries. **The Yuletide Lights of Hope** at The Sutton Place Hotel have been raising funds for the Oak Tree Clinic at BC Children's Hospital for more than a dozen years. The trees are on display from early December to early January.

The **Four Seasons Hotel** (791 West Georgia Street; 604–689–9333) is host to a fund-raising event for the BC Children's Hospital, the **Festival of Trees.** Companies and individuals sponsor trees that are displayed in the hotel lobby from late November to early January. The decorations on the trees range from traditional, with foil and tinsel, to romantic, with ribbons and bows, to vaguely offbeat, but all are an exquisite and fascinating treat to the eyes. In recent years up to thirty-six trees have been in the lobby "forest" for the public to enjoy.

Christmas at Canada Place (999 Canada Place, Cruise Ship Level; recorded message of events, 604–666–8477; proceeds from the $4.00 entrance fee go to children's charities) has been taking place under the sails on the waterfront from early December to early January for more than ten years. Climb onboard the miniature train and chug through a forest of trees and wreaths, all decorated by local businesses. From there see how artistic you can be at the Gingerbread Cookie Decorating Centre. Finish off by rambling through fifteen stages where more than 200 animated characters perform scenes of Christmas.

Hop in the car. Time your arrival at the **VanDusen Botanical Garden** (5251 Oak Street; 604–257–8666; gardens open at 10:00 A.M.; **Festival of Lights** 5:00 P.M. to 9:30 P.M.; $5.00; mid-December to early January; free parking all year) to coincide with the switching on of the lights at 5:00 P.M. Stroll arm in arm through archways of magically suspended lights, past the bowed weeping willows sweeping the sidewalk with necklaces of blue and green illuminating every graceful dip, and the decorative pond and fountains spotted with fantastic colors. The garden is a melee of lights that dress every tree and bush in holiday finery.

Singing Lessons

It's cold outside on the deck of any of the carol ships, but it's your chance to make like Laura and Yuri in Doctor Zhivago *and cozy into your winter clothes, imbibe a hot mulled wine, and sing your hearts out.*

There is something timelessly romantic about warbling to your loved one even if the seagulls do flee at your first note. A time honored tactic of desperation is to lip-sync to the music. For added sincerity, look deeply into your partner's eyes as you do this. With a crowd around, your secret is safe—at least until next Christmas when your lover wants an encore sans boat.

EVENING

Dinner

More than thirty years ago, one lone boat was spruced up with Christmas lights and cruised the waterways around Vancouver. Now the **Carol Ships Parade of Lights Society** (call for information and the schedule; 604–878–9988) has more than one hundred boats from local marinas cruising in its light-festooned boat parade, the crews and passengers singing Christmas carols, on numerous nights throughout December. The ships sail past marinas in False Creek, Burrard Inlet, Coal Harbour, Port Moody, Indian Arm, and Bowen Island, and a local radio station broadcasts the carols, so passengers on the boats and revelers onshore can all join in. And they do. Huge bonfires are lit on land to respond as the boats pass, and hundreds go down to the shore to sing and watch. At the end of the evening, when everyone is tired and quiet, the boats cruise home as a ghostly flotilla of lights in the mist.

Vancouver Champagne Cruises Inc. (100–1676 Duranleau Street, Granville Island; 604–688–8072; dinner cruise, $50) can take you out aboard one of its boats, feed you dinner with all the trimmings, and give you an opportunity to sing to the city. Budding divas wouldn't dare miss this chance. Champagne Cruises' ships depart from Granville Island.

FOR MORE ROMANCE

If you choose not to have dinner on the cruise ship, go Cajun at **Mulvaney's** (1535 Johnston Street, Creek House 9, Granville Island; 604–685–6571; $16 to $24) before joining the carol ship. Hot and spicy Cajun dishes will warm your throat for the evening's entertainment. Although a wide variety of tempting foods are offered, we're particularly fond of most of the blackened dishes, and the Arctic char—a rare treat if you can get it—is the best in the city.

ITINERARY 19
One day

SYMPHONY OF FIRE

A multicolored blast of lights bursts in the sky and reflects on the water. A heavy thump pounds your chest, and loud classical music sounds in your ears. The traffic is still, and a million eyes are watching. The oohs and ahhs are clearly audible for miles along the waterfront. It must be summer in Vancouver during the annual fireworks competition.

Practical notes: This will be a late night, so don't book up your whole day. You'll want to be awake enough to appreciate the fireworks.

AFTERNOON
Lunch

Make your way to the SeaBus Terminal at the corner of Seymour and Cordova Streets. The **SeaBus** (transit information, 604–521–0400; $2.25; runs every fifteen minutes) crosses the harbor in twelve minutes and ends in North Vancouver at the foot of Lonsdale Avenue, and it is the cheapest way to see the inner harbor from the water. As you exit the facility, just follow your nose to your right to the **Lonsdale Quay,** featuring a wide assortment of fresh food stalls; bakeries; eateries of all descriptions, from pubs to fine-dining establishments; and bookstores, crafts shops, and a few upscale clothing stores. If the day is sunny, pick up a scrumptious French loaf at the bakery at the street end of the market, **French Bakery and Pastry Boutique** (123 Carrie Cates Court; 604–987–0227). With some cheeses you can make a picnic out on the boardwalk and admire the city skyline. On rainy days you can cozy up for a light lunch at the **Q Café** (Lonsdale Quay, third floor on the sea side of the building; 604–986–6111). Even with a rain-soaked view, the atmosphere is pleasant and the salads, sandwiches, breads, and soups are tantalizing ($8 to $12).

Or for typical pub fare, the **Water Front Bistro** (one floor down from the Q Café on the water side; 604–986–6111; $6 to $12) serves salads, burgers, nachos, and the like. Our favorite place to eat in the area is **Anatoli Souvlaki** (5 Lonsdale Avenue, North Vancouver; 604–985–9853) for Greek food. Exit the market on the land side, and trundle up Londsdale Avenue (1 block east of the quay). As Greek restaurants go, this is one of the best. The two of you can share one of the Greek Platters for Two for a sample of a little of everything—hummus, spanakopita, dolmathes, Greek salad, and a choice of several meat and fish dishes. The platter is not on the regular lunch menu, but if you ask, the staff will happily put one together for you.

Romance at a Glance

♥ *Admire Vancouver from the SeaBus (604–521–0400).*

♥ *Explore Lonsdale Quay and have a waterfront lunch at the market.*

♥ *Visit the secondhand and antiques stores along lower Lonsdale Avenue.*

♥ *Cruise out to enjoy the Symphony of Fire (604–738–4304).*

♥ *Have a nightcap at Cascades Lounge and watch the boats come home (604–662–8111).*

❧

After lunch if you want to walk along the waterfront, go past the SeaBus terminal and just follow the brick path. The area is a mix of marinas, tugboat facilities, and heavy industry. There's even a sea rescue school where you can watch the training through floor-to-ceiling windows. Or continue up Lonsdale Avenue and explore the shops in the area. In the past few years, several secondhand and antiques stores have been drawn to the area and you never know what you might find. After shopping, wander back over to the SeaBus to return to the Vancouver side. Allow an hour to get from the Lonsdale Quay to Coal Harbor, where the boat departs for tonight's fireworks cruise.

EVENING

Each year corporate sponsors put on a fireworks competition that draws competitive teams from all over the world. China, Spain, the United States and the United Kingdom have been recent competitors. The **Symphony of Fire** (604–738–4304) contest is usually spread over three nights at the end of July and the beginning of August, with the Grande Finale usually on August 5 or 6. A barge is parked in English Bay between English Bay Beach and Kits Beach to launch the rockets safely. By 6:00 P.M. of the contest night, roads leading into parts of the West End, Kits Point, Jericho Beach, and Stanley Park—favored viewing areas— are closed. Traffic along much of the seashore slows to a crawl, and restaurants with a view of the bay fill to capacity as people filter toward the ocean. Darkness doesn't come until after 10:00 P.M., but crowds line the shore out as far as Point Grey and Spanish Banks well before the appointed time. The fireworks are choreographed to music, usually a classical piece, and one of the local radio stations airs it so that anyone with a radio can listen. There are so many radios that one can stand anywhere along the foreshore and hear the rendition.

The pyrotechnics are most impressive from the launching barge and anyone who has a boat crowds out into the bay to surround it. On the water, yet at a safe distance from the barge, you'll feel the visceral thumps of the explosions of light and sound overhead. It's one of the most exciting ways to see the show. Hug each other closely.

Dinner

Charters are available from dozens of sightseeing craft, but reservations are a must if you want to see the fireworks from the water. Try **ABC Boat Charters** (departs from Coal

Harbor, north of the West End near Stanley Park; 604–685–1584; approximately $50 per person, including dinner) for a four- to five-hour cruise that boards at 7:00 P.M. The sunset dinner cruise arrives back at about midnight. Since the cruise leaves from the harbor, you'll get a bit of a tour of the harbor plus the Alaska-bound cruise ships parked nearby from the water, as well as a trip around Stanley Park and under Lions Gate Bridge. Wear layers—it can get cool on the water, and your special companion's body warmth will only take you so far.

Afterward have a drink at the **Cascades Lounge** in the Pan Pacific Hotel (300–999 Canada Place; 604–662–8111) and watch the boats crawl back into port.

FOR MORE ROMANCE

As an alternative for those who hate leaving shore, have dinner at **Cloud Nine Restaurant,** the award-winning revolving restaurant at the top of the Empire Landmark Hotel (1400 Robson Street; 604–687–0511, entrees $20 to $35). Every seat has a terrific view, as the restaurant makes a complete circle about once an hour. The menu is heavy on meats and seafood (there is one vegetarian dish), and one of the most popular dishes is a tender, succulent prime rib. Scallop lovers should try the pan-seared scallops and prawns roasted in pumpkin seed pesto. The cream of squash soup laced with amaretto and roasted almonds was a hit with us, as were the crab and corn fritters with braised leeks and a red pepper and olive oil coulis for an appetizer. Plan your arrival to make sure you're still lingering at the table when the festivities start. This is the ultimate ringside seat.

ITINERARY 20
Two days and one night

ALPINE NIRVANA: WHISTLER

*H*armony and Ptarmigan, Tokum and Bear Paw—these are the incantations and mantras of snow riders bound for the upper reaches and runs of Whistler and Blackcomb Mountains in Whistler. In this place the whispering whiteness of the back bowls will work their magic on the two of you as you stand side by side before the great plunge down the mountain. You couldn't have come to a better setting for romance.

For several years running Whistler has won accolades as the best ski resort in North America. Set in the stupendous scenery of the Coast Mountains with eroded volcanoes all around, the village contains Old European touches throughout. Twenty-five years ago you could still ski in denim and a garbage bag to keep dry, and half the fun was the trip up the avalanche-prone, pretzel highway to the sole chairlift. If you survived sitting on an exposed chair suspended in the subzero chill (Fahrenheit *and* centigrade) for the hour-long ride, you were treated to glorious powder and the freshest air on the planet.

The powder and air are still draws, but the chill has been tamed with new high-speed quad chairs and gondolas, restaurant facilities in which to sip cappuccino at perfect viewing points, and an extensive trail system—the largest in North America—that keeps you moving. The clientele is upscale and cosmopolitan now, and instead of Campbell soup and American cheese slices on white as the special of the day, you can find high-quality fare from many nations. The atmosphere is upbeat and friendly, and only the convalescing are not smiling—unless, of course, they're in one of the many bars and pubs at the base of the mountain.

Practical notes: Even with the terrific improvements of the past decade, Highway 99 to Whistler is not a route to drive for the first time in a night snowstorm. As an alternative, **BC Rail** has scheduled service to Whistler from its North Vancouver Station (1311 West First, North Vancouver; 604–984–5246; reservations recommended; departs from Vancouver at 7:00 A.M. daily, arriving at 9:30 A.M. and returns from Whistler at 6:10 P.M. daily, arriving in Vancouver at 8:45 P.M.; $60 fare round-trip), and taxis can run you into the village cheaply from the terminal. Buses (**Maverick Coach Lines;** 604–662–8051; $32 round-trip) from Vancouver can also drop you in the center of the village. After that you can walk most places easily. For tickets good for skiing at both **Blackcomb** and **Whistler Mountains,** call (604) 932–3434 (the dual mountain pass is $59).

DAY ONE: MORNING

You can check in before skiing or after at the **Chateau Whistler Resort** (4599 Chateau Boulevard, Whistler; 604–938–8000; $170 to $1200, depending on the season, type of room, and special promotions that may be available; there are

Romance Packages), one of the world's top one-hundred hotels, according to a respected travel survey. The hotel was built recently and is the crowning jewel of the hotels at Whistler. Filled with antiques and constructed on a grand scale, it nonetheless manages to perpetuate the illusion of a country ski lodge, with its muted tones, hand-painted leaves and vines on the ceiling, roaring lobby fireplace, and dark wood accents.

With good weather skiing is the choice activity this morning. Drive up early to catch the beginning of the ski day and take a long break for lunch to savor an extra espresso and linger over the top-of-the-world view from Whistler Mountain. Every run is magnificent when you feel your body finely balanced on your skis, floating through a white world like a snow gazelle.

If the upper mountain is not blessed with sparkling weather, the valley also shelters still vistas that are best reached on cross-country skis or by snowshoe. A day of snowshoeing or cross-country skiing around the village will give you a guiltless claim on a sumptuous dessert later while allowing you a bit of quiet conversation while you exercise. Rent snowshoes at **Canadian Snowshoe Adventures** (604–932–0647; staff will drop off your equipment at the hotel in the morning and pick it up in the afternoon; $15 per day rental, or take a guided tour, starting at $19), or outfit yourself for cross-country skiing at **Mountain Adventure Centre** in the Pan Pacific Hotel (beside the Blackcomb gondola in the village; 604–905–2295; $30 a day for all the gear). You can cross-country ski (**Lost Lake Country Trails;** 604–938–7275; $10 a day) on the 30 kilometers of trails around one of the golf courses, Lost Lake, and the Chateau Whistler.

Nonskiers will find skating, snowmobiling, swimming, or other sports in which to excel. Shopping in Whistler's high-class collection of clothing and art shops has left more than one visitor with a deep well in their credit card account. As in any other world-class resort, stacks of overpriced goods beckon you, but also there are unique sculptures and clothing you'd expect to find only on Fifth Avenue in New York or in the Ginza in Tokyo. Window shopping is free, so poke around to your heart's content.

DAY ONE: AFTERNOON

Lunch

If the weather is clear, take a gondola ride to the top of Blackcomb Mountain and have lunch at **Christine's** (604–938–7437; open daily during ski season from 11:30 A.M. to 2:00 P.M.; reservations recommended; entrees $8 to $17; the restaurant will deduct $10 of the cost of your Adult Day Sightseeing Pass from your meal cost, but will not reimburse ski-lift tickets; Christine's is also open during summer on a limited number of evenings for sunset dining, one of the most bewitching and romantic ways to spend a couple of hours). Not only is the food scrumptious and perfectly presented (try the venison and mushroom ragout), but the view of Cougar Mountain, Rainbow Glacier, and the snow-clad Coast Mountain Range from one of the world's highest fine-dining restaurants will take your breath away. The dress code does include ski clothes, so even if you're skiing, you can drop in for a civilized and dignified meal before resuming your afternoon of creating improbable postures in the snow.

DAY ONE: EVENING

Dinner

Since Whistler has attained world-class-resort status, many notable restaurants have opened that cater to the resort's high-energy spirit. Unlike some of the loud busy places in the village, the quiet atmosphere of the **Wildflower Restaurant** on the château's main level gently washes over you and smoothes out the day's wrinkles (entrees $18 to $32). To watch the day fade, sit facing the ski area and the outdoor patio, just to the right of the main entrance to the restaurant. (For a more intimate cocoon, sit toward the back.) If you're there late in the ski season, April or early May, the afternoon light filters in through large windows to give you a glimpse of the outdoor activity. Earlier in the year, when it is assuredly dark during dinner, the stark black and white of the mountain lit by floodlights is a cold counter-point to the warm blue, crimson, and mustard decor of the restaurant's hospitable haven. Many of the pieces that contribute to the rustic adornment you see around you were saved from the demolition of a heritage church in Quebec.

Whatever you choose to eat, the service will be attentive but not overbearing and the food well presented and delicious. But we do have a favorite: The restaurant is justifiably proud of its Asian Buffet ($35), served only on Friday and Saturday nights. You'll delight in cracked crab and other seafoods, wok-seared veggies, and fried dim sum, but don't miss the Nasi Goreng (Malaysian fried rice). Wash it all down with Chinese Tsing Tao, Japanese Asahi Super Dry, or Indian Kingfisher beer.

⊙↓⊙

After dinner take a horse-drawn sleigh ride through the mountain woods just above the village. Bundling together under a blanket while whisking through the crystal night air with the village lights below you is magical regardless of how many people join the ride (**Blackcomb Horsedrawn Sleigh Rides Inc.;** 604–932–7631; rides depart at 5:00, 6:30, and 8:00 P.M.; $45 per person; the enterprise is near the Chateau Whistler, but call and ask for exact directions).

Especially if it's snowing, take advantage of the outdoor pool and hot tub at the Chateau's spa (open until 11:00 P.M.). You can start with a sauna to warm you and proceed outside by dipping into the heated pool indoors and swimming out. Sitting in the hot tub, watching the lights of the hotel flicker through the haze of warm fog and snowflakes, is a dreamy way to end a day on the mountain. After padding back to your room via the secret passages of the third-floor route (ask the spa desk personnel how to get to your room without going through the lobby) dress casually and make your way down to the **Mallard Bar** (604–938–8000) for a nightcap. The pleasant piano, comfy wingback chairs, dim light, and fireplace are guaranteed to soften your demeanor as you gaze at the snow falling outside.

For those who never sleep, the village offers plenty of nightlife. Try dancing and pool at **Buffalo Bill's** (4122 Village Green; 604–932–6613; open daily noon to 2:00 A.M. except Sunday). You can dance the night away, but be warned: Morning-after regret has claimed more than one dancing skier who has not had the stamina to ski the next day.

DAY TWO: MORNING
Breakfast

For breakfast you can, of course, order room service. But if you're ready to get out and face the day, walk over to **Auntie Em's Kitchen** (as in *The Wizard of Oz*'s Auntie Em) in the new village for a pre-ski feast (129–4340 Lorimer Road in the Village North Marketplace; 604–932–1163; open 6:30 A.M. to 6:00 P.M.; $6 to $7). It's one the few places in Whistler that serves breakfast all day. Waffles with strawberries or blueberries and whipped cream (more healthful alternatives are on the menu, including sugarless items for those who must deprive themselves), all kinds of eggs, homemade breads and pastries, and croissant melts are hugely popular. For a quick start order a breakfast burrito, a tortilla shell filled with your choice of ingredients, and one of the fresh-squeezed juice combos. Round out your pre-ski fueling with a bolt of imported Italian coffee.

As an alternative, try **Crepe Montagne** (116–4368 Main Street in the Market Pavilion; 604–905–4444; 8:00 A.M. to 10:00 P.M.; $3 to $10) for breakfast, where Laurence and Michel Gagnon will prepare a superb crepe for you and you can practice your French. Although this breakfast spot in the village does serve other breakfast items, such as waffles, its claim to fame is the crepe selection. You can have a breakfast crepe of ham, bacon, eggs, and cheese at any time of day, so you can make a slow start and let all the skiers rush off to the slopes before you venture out.

DAY TWO: AFTERNOON

Lunch

On the off chance that one of you decides to ski and the other wants to rest (or read, or shop), **Monk's Grill** (4555 Blackcomb Way; 604–932–9677; $5 to $12) is the perfect meeting place for lunch. It's only a block from the chateau, at the bottom of one of the runs on Blackcomb Mountain, so the more athletic of the two of you can ski in and, after lunch, ski out. The food is hearty fare, such as Southern fried chicken, burgers with dual patties and Canadian Cheddar cheese (of course!), and pizzas. Those not carbo-loading can order the grilled chicken and spiced pecan salad with orange sesame vinaigrette, but don't expect to excel at shushing the slopes for the whole afternoon on such beneficial nourishment—good old-fashioned fat and calories fit well with the carefree, upbeat, and busy atmosphere. The restaurant, especially on a sunny day on the patio, where suntanning is still considered healthy, is just what you'd expect of a world-class ski resort.

◈◈

For an afternoon break from skiing, if the day is sunny and the roads are clear, take a drive into the surrounding developments. Residents, especially the newest ones, are frantically building Whistler into a showcase of alpine splendor. Million-dollar houses designed by name architects are everywhere, and even simple shacks owned by old-timers are worth more than the same lot in the already high-priced Vancouver real estate market. When you can cull the rich and famous from seven continents, there doesn't seem to be an upper limit on spending. Logs and glass are popular construction materials but you can find almost anything. For a little longer drive, head north on Highway 99 to **Pemberton,** where the mountains are steeper and seem to hang menacingly above you. Spectacular and scary!

In spring, when the weather is warmer, grazing and sipping the day away or just table-hopping from one restaurant to another is a time-honored tradition at Whistler. Start at **Aviano**

Summer at Whistler

There's plenty to do in summer around Whistler. Hordes descend to hike Singing Pass or paddle the creeks and rivers around the village. As with any resort destination, there's always someone who, for a price, can offer you an experience you won't normally find in the big city. You can travel the backroads on horseback, on all-terrain vehicles, or with llamas; paddle the rivers and creeks in canoes, inflatable rafts, or kayaks; or hike lonely trails with a guide or walk lush golf courses.

But the best attraction of all is Brandywine Falls, just north of Daisy Lake, the man-made reservoir, on the road up to Whistler. A few kilometers past the dam and lakeshore are blue government-information signs that give you ample warning that the parking lot is near (in winter the lot is sometimes snowed under and the park is closed). Follow the marked trail from the parking area for an easy, five-minute walk to one of the most awesome natural phenomena in the area. At 70 meters, it's not particularly high, but the observation deck puts you right out over the cliffside into the eroded horseshoe of the falls.

Restaurant and Bar (604–932–2112) in Whistler Village Square and grab a front-row seat on the patio facing the square; a constant parade of spectacles will come to you. When it's time to stretch your legs, make a pact that you will amble at least a dozen meters before plunking down in another outdoor restaurant. This gives you a little variety.

FOR MORE ROMANCE

The whole village of Whistler takes Christmas to heart. Gingerbread houses covered in snow, with carolers finding their way by candlelight, really do exist during the holidays. Especially if you stay in one of the subdivisions in a B&B, you'll find singers gathered at your door on the nights before Christmas. Traipsing through pale snow to entice snuggled-in homebodies to brave the cold and come join in the singing isn't some Hollywood fantasy, but you'll swear Bing is in the crowd somewhere.

VANCOUVER ISLAND

STORM WATCHING: TOFINO, VANCOUVER ISLAND

*T*he North Pacific generates terrific storms in the winter. Cold emerald waves from the Orient crash over rocky beaches and fill the air with a fine salt haze you can taste. The coast here is a series of wide sand beaches hemmed by craggy headlands. Stands of primeval Sitka spruce, some 200 feet high, edge the water. Eagles and seals outnumber people, and during early spring the entire world population of gray whales parades past on their annual migration to Alaska.

This is the perfect place for an impassioned love affair. Raw energy is at work here; no room exist for subtle gestures. Walk the beach at low tide and surrender yourself to the storm. After a wild wet walk, curl up in a wingback chair beside your fireplace. As you dry your hair, watch the Pacific rollers shatter on the rocks below your window.

Practical notes: Pack extra clothes and waterproof or extra footwear for this sojourn. Storm-watching season starts in November. In summer the beaches are well used, especially on weekends, but there's still plenty of room. The area has many charter and tour companies, for everything from deep-sea fishing to kayaking to visiting hot springs. The **Tofino Tourism Information Centre** (346 Campbell Street, Tofino; 250–725–3414; open daily early spring to early fall) can guide you to the best places and current costs for what you want to do. This trip can easily be combined with any other of the Vancouver Island itineraries.

DAY ONE: LATE MORNING/ EARLY AFTERNOON

Romance at a Glance

♥ *Stay at The Wickaninnish Inn for the best storm watching on the coast (800–333–4604).*

♥ *Treat your palate to a sensuous seafood feast at The Pointe Restaurant (250–725–3100).*

♥ *Beachcomb on Long Beach and snack at the Wickaninnish Restaurant (250–726–7706).*

♥ *Whale-watch with Jamie's Whaling Station (250–725–3919).*

♥ *Dine at the Sea Shanty (800–899–1947) or the Blue Heron Pub (250–725–3277).*

♥ *Enjoy a walk along interpretive trails in the rainforest.*

Lunch

This trip begins with a voyage from the Horseshoe Bay Ferry Terminal to Nanaimo. (See the BC Ferries Appendix for further information; you can also leave from Tsawwassen Terminal). If you arrive early, eat lunch at the **Boathouse Restaurant** (6695 Nelson, Horseshoe Bay; 604–921–8188; open 11:30 A.M. to 9:30 or 10:00 P.M. on weekends; $7 to $12), perched on the end of the dock. The spectacular view of the fjord of Howe Sound is as good as any you'll find in Norway or Patagonia, and watching the ferries dock is a bonus. Although the Boathouse is ostensibly a seafood house, it offers a full range of pastas and other fare, so anyone should be able to find something to soothe a hungry stomach.

❧

You'll need to leave by at least midday Friday to avoid the weekend ferry crush. Although the entire trip takes about six hours, two hours are aboard the car ferry. Pass the time on the stern enticing seagulls coasting in the ferry's wind draft to take bits of bread from your fingers. Be sure to have your camera and a pair of binoculars at hand. Pods of orcas are a common sight along the ferry run, and with patience you might find a seal or two. Anytime you're near shore, scan the tops of trees for eagles; golfers are particularly good at spotting their white headfeathers from a distance.

When you drive off the ferry, stay to your right and the road will take you to Highway 19. Continue out of the town of Nanaimo, toward the city of Parksville and the junction with Highway 4, which crosses the island from east to west. The drive over the Vancouver Island Mountains to Port Alberni and Tofino contains numerous scenic outlooks. Stretch your legs with a short walk in **MacMillan Provincial Park's Cathedral Grove.** The western red cedars (one of the largest trees in North America) and Douglas firs are at least 200 feet tall, and some exceed 500 years of age. If you miss the sign announcing the entrance to the woods, you'll know you're there when you enter a tunnel of towering, pencil-straight trees that come to the very edge of the road. These are the British Columbia equivalent to the giant redwoods of California. At this altitude the temperature may be chilly—which gives you a good reason to stroll the well-groomed paths arm in arm—and the air is always a fragrant blend of pure pine and earthy moss.

On a warm day treat yourself to a swim in one of several lakes that are open to the public for swimming along the road. During fire season you might be entertained by a unique aerial display, as four bright yellow engine water-bombers descend, on the fly, to scoop water from the lakes.

As you approach the ocean, the highway comes to a T junction. Turn right for 15 miles (25 kilometers) to reach the inn where you'll stay during this outing. On the way you'll have teasing glimpses of the Pacific Ocean on your left. For the most stunning introduction, wait until you see the sign for Long Beach—the panorama of the 6-mile strip of white sand, salt spray, giant trees, and fitful ocean is typically West Coast.

Although the Canadian government has stopped development of the beaches area, old-timers have been allowed to develop some of their holdings, under strict control. The most romantic of the numerous B&Bs and inns in this area is **The Wickaninnish Inn** (Osprey Lane at Chesterman Beach, Tofino, BC, V0R 2Z0; 800–333–4604; $120 to $340; ask about Romance Packages), built on a headland just to the north of the park. Look for THE WICKANINNISH INN sign on your left within 1 mile of exiting the park.

The Wickaninnish is a brand-new, 2-story structure of pine and yellow cedar crafted to fit its surroundings perfectly. Each of the forty-six rooms in the inn has a west-facing view of the ocean or beach and double soaker tubs with large picture windows looking out to sea. (There is a drop-down blind, but only the fish will see you if you don't use it.) Handcrafted soap produced locally and fluffy robes await you as a special treat, and scented candles are supplied. In the main room two wingback chairs face two more large windows on either side of the fireplace. In winter the room offers the perfect cocoon for curling up with a good book and hot chocolate when an intense storm is raging outside. In summer you can use the balcony chairs to watch for the steam as the sun sizzles into the sea at sunset.

Ask one of the owners, Charles or Doug, to tell you the story about the pictures of the Chilean ship *Carelmapu* that grace the lobby. During a brutal storm in the winter of 1915, the *Carelmapu* foundered offshore in full view of the passengers and crew of a nearby passenger steamer, the *Princess Maquinna,* who were helpless to do anything to aid. Despite rescue attempts, all but five of the crew eventually drowned. The whole area is a graveyard for hundreds of ships and sailors, and the paintings by a local artist capture the drama and danger of the coast admirably. If you stand on the beach below the inn and look out to sea on a stormy day, you can almost hear the frantic calls of some of the sailors trapped offshore aboard the doomed *Carelmapu.*

DAY ONE: EVENING
Dinner

The Pointe Restaurant (dinner entrees $19 to $34) in the inn is already famous along the coast for the chef's creations. Pick a time for dinner reservations when you first reserve your room, because many evenings the place is completely sold out. Although the restaurant is upscale, dress is West Coast casual (only shorts and T-shirts are banned for dinner). Everyone should try the salmon, which is a British Columbia specialty and is prepared in a dozen

different ways. When in season, the relatively rare Arctic char is always any fish aficionado's first choice. No matter what you choose, leave room for dessert. The selection is not large, but it is rich and sensual. (Be assured that all calories have been painstakingly removed by hand.)

❧

The beach at low tide is also a must on a rainless night. Get a flashlight from the front desk to negotiate the steps to the beach, and then switch it off. Stand still with your back to the lights of the inn and wait. In a few minutes billions of stars will appear. Every few minutes you'll see the glittering streaks of meteors. With the music of the sea for accompaniment, this can be a religious experience.

DAY TWO: MORNING
Breakfast

Breakfast in the round, glass-enclosed Pointe Restaurant ($5 to $11) dining room shouldn't be missed. The view is so expansive, with so much happening—seals, seabirds, crashing waves—that you can spend hours watching. The menu has a wide assortment of appetizing breakfasts for both nibblers and lumberjacks. Some of the freshly squeezed juice concoctions are unique—try the watermelon-and-mango if it's offered.

❧

After breakfast go for a walk along **Chesterman Beach.** If the tide is low, you can walk out to **Frank Island,** directly in front of the beach, but be sure you time the tides right. Ask at the front desk for advice. You don't want to be trapped for six hours. The inn provides bright yellow, good-quality raingear so that you can stay relatively dry, but it's a bet that at some point in exploring tidal pools, you'll soak your feet. Take a pair of knee-high rubber boots or extra sneakers to change into.

DAY TWO: AFTERNOON

The whole region is a maze of waterways, estuaries, and islands, and an exploration by water can cheerfully fill an afternoon. During spring and summer and particularly during whale-watching season, you can board a variety of small boats to go out among the whales.

At the peak of whale-watching season, from early March to mid-April, you can see whales from along the shore and in the bays, but if you want to take a boat ride, be sure to call ahead for reservations. The cost averages $30 to $35 per person. **Whalefest** takes place along the coast from **Ucluelet** to **Tofino** from March 7 to April 15; call the Ucluelet Chamber of Commerce for an events calendar (250–726–4641).

Small inflatable boats and converted Coast Guard rescue boats will give you a thrilling ride out to the whales and allow you to move in extremely close to the leviathans. Protective clothing is provided. Don't take your best camera unless you know how to wrap it to protect it from the salt spray. Disposable and inexpensive pocket cameras are the order of the day.

More sedate trips can be mounted with some of the larger boats of the West Coast fleet. **Jamie's Whaling Station** (on the waterfront in Tofino; 250–725–3919) has the only glass-bottom boat, and on a lucky day you might see whales swimming underneath. Jamie's can also provide a thrilling experience in 23-foot rigid hull inflatables fitted with two big engines.

These wave runners promise a wet roller-coaster ride that's the fastest way to get to and from wherever the whales have been spotted that day.

Lunch

Lunch is served onboard some of the larger vessels, and both Tofino and Ucluelet have cafes worth visiting if you need sustenance before boarding. Try the **Common Loaf Bake Shop** (180 First Street, Tofino; 250–725–3915) for an alternative menu of breads, baked goods, sweets, and coffee and tea, or the **Alleyway Café** (305 Campbell Street, Tofino, behind the bank; 250–725–3105), which creates vegetarian fantasies.

If you're in the area between early spring and fall, however, try the **Wickaninnish Restaurant** (south end of Long Beach—watch for a sign along the highway just after you enter the Pacific Rim National Park; 250–726–7706), at the Canadian government interpretive center right on the beach. The stone fireplace, open-beam construction, and all-around glass make this a spectacular place for a repast. As you would expect, the menu is mostly seafood, which is fairly well done.

❦

After lunch, if you have time before your afternoon outing, kick a little sand on the beach. The premium prize for any beachcomber is the green-tinted-glass globes that Japanese fishers use with their nets. Finding one that has made its way all the way across the Pacific is considered to be extremely lucky. Also finding a pair of expensive basketball shoes washed ashore would be akin to winning the lottery. Ever since a container of top-of-the-line brand-name sneaks washed overboard off the coast a few years ago, they have been appearing singly. Many flea markets have an array of mismatched shoes looking for mates. Finding a pair at the same time would probably qualify you for a round of drinks at the local pub. Your treat, of course.

When you arrive back at the wharf in Tofino after your trip on the water, spend time exploring. The village center has a number of galleries and gift shops featuring Native art from local carvers and painters, as well as some superb crafts. You can't miss the **Eagle Aerie Galley** (800–663–0669) because it's in an eye-catching Northwest Coast First Nation–style longhouse situated, as you come into town, on your right (the corner of Second and Campbell). It features original limited-edition carvings and paintings. **House of Himwitsa** (300 Main Street; 250–725–2017) has an extensive collection of Native carvings, totems, paintings, jewelry, and pottery. The company and the complex are all First Nation–owned.

Day Two: Evening
Dinner

The **Sea Shanty** (300 Main Street; 800–899–1947; $10 to $19) is on the waterfront near the government dock in Tofino, and from the patio you can watch the seaplanes, fishing boats, and other assorted traffic, including an occasional whale. The menu is Northwest Coast cuisine, with an emphasis on seafood but with a French twist. Fresh shrimp, oysters, and crab feasts with all the trimmings; creamy seafood pastas; seafood sandwiches—all are good values and tasty.

If the Sea Shanty is closed for the season, try the **Blue Heron Pub,** at the Weigh West Marine Resort (634 Campbell Street; 250–725–3277; $7 to $15). In addition to the typical pub fare of nachos, chicken wings, fish-and-chips, and hamburgers (try the Blue Heron Burger: terrific!) are a variety of other dishes, such as seafood pastas and tortillas wraps. The dinner menu in winter is more extensive and includes steaks, baby back ribs, and crab feasts. The restaurant is on the harbor, and its glass wall gives you both a splendid view and local color—loggers, fishermen, artists, craftspeople, and more.

DAY THREE: MORNING

On your way back to Vancouver, you might want to limber up with a walk along the coast rainforest interpretive trails in the Pacific Rim National Forest. Signs along the highway within the park alert you to where to go. The moss covering absolutely everything along the two 1-kilometer trails will amaze you and impart a sense of what several feet of rain per year does in a temperate rainforest.

FOR MORE ROMANCE

Those who prefer the personal touch of a B&B have a treat in store for them. Also on Chesterman Beach within walking distance of the Wickaninnish Inn is **Chesterman's Beach Bed and Breakfast** (1345 Chesterman's Beach road, Tofino; 250–725–3726; $125 to $195). Each of the three rooms has its own charm, and each is romantic in its own way. The Garden Cottage is separate from the house and affords you a little more privacy and a private garden, while the other two rooms have an ocean view (the Garden Cottage does not). The Ocean Spray Room has French doors, a fireplace, and a private sauna, while in the Lookout Suite you can actually lie in the four-poster bed and watch the waves roll in almost to the door.

WHAT'S OLD IS NEW AGAIN:
VICTORIA, VANCOUVER ISLAND

Kipling's Victoria

"To realize Victoria you must take all that the eye admires in Bournemouth, Torquay, the Isle of Wight, the happy valley at Hong Kong, the Doon, Sorrento and Camp's Bay—add reminiscences of the Thousand Islands and arrange the whole around the Bay of Naples with some Himalayas for the background." —*Rudyard Kipling*

*I*t's hard to remain sophisticated and debonair when your dinner keeps sliding into your lap and champagne splashes your face. Or so thought the general director of the Canadian Pacific Railway Company. His dinner cars swayed and slid as the engines tried to pull the heavily loaded trains up the steep inclines of the Rocky Mountains.

As a solution, he built the first Canadian Pacific Hotels, simple Alps-style chalets along the tracks at some of the more spectacular points. As their reputation as an oasis in the wilderness made them more popular, the general director's plans became more grandiose, culminating in the majestic architecture of the Banff Springs (1888), the Chateau Lake Louise (1890), and the jewel of the Pacific wilderness, The Empress (1908).

Though a colonist might have spent most of the year battling the hardships of the hinterland, when he or she arrived in Victoria and entered the lobby of The Empress, it was clear that there was still a civilized world and all was right with the Empire. While you and your loved one needn't endure the same battle to reach The Empress, the enjoyment you'll experience will be no less than that of the colonists of old.

Practical notes: You can easily do this itinerary without a car, since everything is either within walking distance or a short taxi ride away. Some of the antiques shops are open Sunday during summer, while others are closed Sunday year-round. When it comes to clothes, much of the west coast is very casual, and even The Empress has relaxed its standards; however, be advised that when you are "taking tea," no ripped jeans, short-shorts, tank tops, or jogging suits are allowed. Indeed. For information contact **Tourism Victoria,** 812 Wharf Street, Victoria, BC, V8W 1T3 (250–953–2033).

Romance at a Glance

♥ *Enter a world of gracious living at The Empress (800–441–1414 or 250–384–8111).*

♥ *Relax over lunch at Sam's Deli (250–382–8424).*

♥ *Window-shop or worse on Antique Row.*

♥ *Slowly sip afternoon tea in The Empress's Tea Lobby.*

♥ *Listen to live music in The Empress's Bengal Lounge.*

♥ *Tour the city on the top of a red double-decker bus (250–388–5248).*

DAY ONE:
LATE MORNING/EARLY AFTERNOON

You can take your car to the Tsawwassen Ferry terminal, but we suggest you make your way to the Vancouver Bus Terminal

(1150 Station Street, Vancouver; 800–661–1725 or 604–662–8074) for a hassle-free bus ride over. The Pacific Coach Line (800–661–1725 or 250–385–4411) will take you onto the ferry and into Victoria in about three and a half hours. The Victoria Bus Terminal (700 Douglas Street, Victoria) is right behind The Empress hotel; you won't be able to miss it.

The Empress (721 Government Street, Victoria; 800–441–1414 or 250–384–8111; from $140 double) is centrally located right on the harborfront, kitty-corner from the Provincial Parliament Buildings, across from the Royal British Columbia Museum and the shopping district. This landmark property has been renovated in the past ten years to restore it to its charming former glory.

As you enter the pink and gray stone walls of The Empress, have a last look around outside before you check in, for once you've entered The Empress, you may not want to surface for a while—you can easily spend your whole visit here without leaving the premises. Between the pool, the whirlpool, the wade pool, the sauna and exercise room, the shopping, afternoon tea in the Tea Lobby (a several-hours affair), drinks in the Bengal Lounge, lunch in Kipling's, and formal dining in The Empress Dining Room, your time could be quite full. We suggest you splurge and check into a Harbor View Room on the Entrée Gold floor. With Entrée Gold you'll have access to private check-in, a private lounge where you'll be able to get tea and coffee at any time of the day, full continental breakfast in the morning, hors d'oeuvres in the afternoon, and even a shoeshine if you want it. Or for a slightly different view of the world, ask for one of the Attic rooms; they tend to be smaller, but are cozy and full of character. To access these rooms, one takes the elevator up to the sixth floor and then walks up a flight of stairs to the seventh. Odd, yes, but these rooms were in fact the old servants' quarters. Room 730 is one of the larger Attic Rooms and has the best view of the harbor. Try for an early check-in if you arrive late in the morning, or stash your bags with the concierge while you shop for antiques.

Promising Start

The Empress has seen thousands of honeymoons and marriage proposals and the promises that go with them, but few like this. A couple who recently checked in explained that the groom was simply fulfilling a promise to his bride that they would honeymoon at The Empress. The wedding had taken place in 1928 and the couple went camping right after the wedding, not the official honeymoon, of course. Finally, at age 103 the man took his 92-year-old bride to a suite at The Empress and fulfilled his promise. This has to be a record for foreplay.

Lunch

As you leave the hotel and are facing the harbor, turn to your right. Cross Humboldt Street and the first place you come to on the right-hand side is **Sam's Deli** (805 Government Street, Victoria; 250–382–8424; $7 to $12). The sandwiches are enormous, and the soups are as good as Mother ever made. (Prices are reasonable—$14 for two hungry people.) You may want to share a plate to save plenty of room for snacks along the way later in the afternoon. This is the heart of the downtown area and the entrance to shoppers' heaven, so the crowd-watching is excellent.

⊙↑⊙

Now hide your wallets from yourselves and go forth to Fort Street, a thoroughfare popularly known as **Antique Row.** In the first antiques shop you see, go in and ask the staff if they have a brochure called *Victoria's Antique Shops;* it's a guide to twenty-six antiques dealers in the downtown area and the kind of merchandise they offer. If the first shop doesn't have one, just wander along and you'll see the stores as you go. The thick of the offerings is in the 1000 block, with the Tudor-front shops. One shop we like is **David Robinson Ltd.**

(1023 Fort Street, Victoria; 250–384–6425), which specializes in period furniture, clocks, Oriental rugs, and porcelain. To track down discontinued patterns of silver flatware, visit **Classic Silverware** (1033 Fort Street, Victoria; 250–383–6860).

Also there are a couple of malls housing large numbers of small dealers with varied goods. The **Vanity Fair Antique Mall** (1044 Fort Street; 250–380–7274; open 10:00 A.M. to 5:30 P.M. and Sunday 11:00 A.M. to 4:00 P.M. all year), with more than forty dealers, offers antiques, collectibles, and books. Or ramble through **Recollections Antique and Collectible Mall** (817A Fort Street, Victoria; 250–385–1902; open Monday through Saturday 10:00 A.M. to 6:00 P.M. and Sunday 11:00 A.M. to 4:00 P.M. all year), which has more than fifty dealers.

When your feet lag, head back for the time-honored "afternoon tea."

DAY ONE: EARLY EVENING
Afternoon Tea

People argue that you can't say you've experienced Victoria unless you've had afternoon tea at The Empress. Who are we to disagree? Though a number of other places offer afternoon tea, none do so with the history that comes with this hotel. So tidy up and mosey on down to the lobby.

Afternoon tea is served in the **Tea Lobby** among the flowers, either looking out on the harbor or under the stained-glass dome of the **Palm Court**—in summertime on the **Verandah**—and runs from 12:30 to 5:00 P.M. We suggest reserving when you book your room so that you'll be sure to get the time you want, especially if you're traveling in summer (250–384–8111 or 800–441–1414; $19.95 November to March and $29.00 during summer).

We suggest a high (late) tea so you'll have plenty of time to explore Fort Street, and unless you have a firm grip on your appetite, it will probably replace dinner for you. You'll get a china rack laden with smoked salmon, deviled egg, cucumber, and watercress (would it really be tea without cucumber and watercress?) sandwiches; scones; and preserves and thick clotted cream. And then there are the pastries and fruit and seasonal berries to finish. The tea itself is poured from silver pots into delicate china teacups, your choice of the best blends made from China black, Darjeeling, and Ceylon teas. So sit back, sip gracefully, and enjoy the soft background music and the sound of your loved one's voice as you share this very traditional teatime.

DAY ONE: EVENING

The **Bengal Lounge** (250–384–8111; various buffets, $12.50 to $18.00) is a throwback to a tropical colony during the early part of the century, with its huge palm trees, ceiling fans, dark wood pillars, Oriental carpets, wicker, and overstuffed chairs. Relax and have a drink while you listen to the live music. Be warned: despite the filling afternoon tea, if you're there on a night the lounge is serving dinner (every night during peak season and only Friday and

Saturday in off-season), you may be unable to resist the temptation of the wafting spices and you'll have to savor the rich flavors of the famous curries.

A leisurely swim in the glass-enclosed pool and perhaps a little time in the whirlpool will easily put you in the mood for sleep or something else. In summer you can also sit out on the front veranda and watch the night steal over the sky.

DAY TWO: MORNING
Breakfast

Don't let the comfort of the Entrée Gold lounge prevent you from finishing your breakfast and heading out to explore the city. You may be tempted to bury yourself in one of the butter-soft leather wingback chairs, sip your coffee, read the paper or your book—sparing a loving glance at your mate every now and then, of course—and not budge for several hours. But there are things to do.

If you prefer a hot breakfast, or if you haven't chosen the Entrée Gold floor, **Kipling's** (250–384–8111; $12 to 20), named for the famous British author Rudyard Kipling and located downstairs in the hotel, offers plentiful options for breakfast. Or head across the street on the waterfront to **Milestones Inner Harbour** (812 Wharf Street, Victoria; 250–381–2244) for a variety of breakfast choices. This is hearty fare, well seasoned, and the portions are large enough for two people to share. The number one choice of the hungry for breakfast is the Prime Rib Hash. The 1,000-Grain Toast is a tasty meal in itself, and if you can talk the staff into it, the Apple Crumble from the lunch menu is a filling and healthful breakfast of fruit and grains (the sugar and bourbon are just there for a little flavor).

∽

After breakfast see Victoria aboard one of the red British double-decker buses. The ninety-minute tour takes in some of the older, more exclusive neighborhoods; shows you the place where Rudyard Kipling spent his last days; carries you along the beaches overlooking the Strait of Juan de Fuca Islands and the snowcapped Olympic Mountain Range across the channel; and gives you a preview of the shopping areas you'll later visit on foot. Sitting atop a red double-decker bus, holding hands, and looking down on the world while someone else does the driving beat walking or driving yourself.

Catch the **Gray Line** (250–388–5248; $16) double-decker bus right in front of the Empress hotel. The Gray Line's kiosk is a stationary red double-decker bus that you cannot miss. Departures are almost hourly, but schedules do vary a bit depending on the season. Seating is first come, first served, and the best seat is, naturally, on top at the front. Because the view from all seats is good, it may not be worth sitting inside on a warm day while waiting for the rest of the passengers to board.

The bus will drop you back in front of the hotel for your walk to more closely explore some of the shops you passed during the ride. Ask the concierge for a street map before you leave. A good route to follow is along Government Street (go to the right as you are standing in front of the hotel, facing the water) and then turn left onto Fisgard Street (the heart of Victoria's International District), then left again onto Store Street, and carry along on Wharf Street back to the Empress. Take your time and explore some of the shops en route.

Stop in at **Murchie's** (1110 Government Street, Victoria; 250–383–3112), the 100-year-old company that's responsible for the Empress's tea. What better souvenir to take home to remind yourselves of this visit to the past? In the 1300 block of Government Street is **The Original Christmas Village Store** (250–380–7522), with four levels of thousands of Christmas collectibles and treasures. Squeeze your way along **Fan Tan Alley,** Canada's narrowest shopping alley (only two shoulder-widths wide), in the block between Pandora and Fisgard. The **Fan Tan Gallery** (541 Fisgard Street, Victoria; 250–382–4424) is a great spot to shop for glassware, masks, woven goods, baskets, candles, and some original art. Art lovers will want to stop at **Dales Gallery** (537 Fisgard Street, Victoria; 250–383–1552) for originals and prints done by local artists such as Grant Fuller, whose watercolors capture the spirit of the West Coast perfectly.

The main entrance to **Market Square** (250–386–2441; most stores open daily 10:00 A.M. to 5:00 P.M.) is on Johnston Street. Market Square is a series of heritage buildings that were renovated and turned into shops and cafes, with about forty-five retailers of all sorts of paraphernalia, some kitsch and some not. The open area between the buildings serves as an outdoor courtyard for jazz performances and special events. Grab a drink from one of the vendors and rest your feet while you people-watch.

FOR MORE ROMANCE

Just to remind you, The Empress has Romantic Getaway Packages ($145 Canadian) that will give you a horse-drawn carriage tour, wine, a trivet, and breakfast, and the package can be added to any room arrangements.

ITINERARY 23
Two days and one night

PLEASE, EAT THE DAISIES:
SOOKE, VANCOUVER ISLAND

*A*s a child, you no doubt had your hand slapped in the nick of time as you tried to sample the world with your mouth. Hmmm—the yellow flowers look particularly tasty today, but are they as good as this marigold-yellow crayon? Well, here's your chance to find out. The celebrated Sooke Harbour House has welcomed refugees from the big city with its innovative blend of local seafood, garden-fresh vegetables, and edible flowers. Here the garnishes are meant to be eaten and are guaranteed to surprise your taste buds. Unless you are an avid gardener yourself or a botanist, half the salad will evoke curiosity. As the head gardener says, "If you can't eat it, we don't grow it."

Practical notes: For general information about the area, contact the **Sooke Region Museum and Visitor Information Centre** (250–642–6351). Take the ferry from Tsawwassen Terminal to Swartz Bay Terminal (see the BC Ferries Appendix for details). The trip to Sooke will take approximately four hours, including the ferry ride, and can be easily combined with other itineraries on Vancouver Island.

DAY ONE: AFTERNOON

The **Sooke Harbour House** (1528 Whiffen Spit Road, Sooke; 250–642–3421; $175 to $465, depending on the season; price includes both breakfast and lunch) is composed of three parts, situated only steps from the water. The older rooms, in the main house, are well appointed with antiques and all the amenities, such as a double soaker tub, fluffy robes, and a fireplace. If you like cozy rooms with nooks and crannies, ask for Room 1 in the original house. Built on two levels, the bath and bed are set into dormers. The bathroom serves as the foyer, with a double-pedestal partner's desk as the sink and a double soaker tub under the window. You may have guessed that this bathroom is more akin to a Roman bath than the normal North American model is.

The choice room at the inn is the Victor Newman Room, partly because of the layout but also because of all the terrific Coast Indian art. The Victor Newman Room is a more

Romance at a Glance

♥ *Let your senses roam at the Sooke Harbour House (250–642–3421).*

♥ *Frolic in the Sooke Potholes.*

♥ *Take a whiff of Whiffen Spit.*

♥ *Explore the West Coast village of Sooke.*

modern open plan than Room 1. The two-sided fireplace in the middle of the room warms the sitting area with its double hand-carved rocking chair and also covers with its warm glow the cedar-wrapped double soaker tub on the other side. The soaker tub is built of polished cedar, which reflects the fireplace in such a way as to make it seem that the two of you are in a pool of fire. The room also has twenty pieces of original Native art, including a 5-foot carving of a stylized whale with movable fins and mouth.

The rooms are designed to open widely to the outdoors and take full advantage of the view. Nestling in the quilts with the door open to capture the sound of the breaking waves below and seeing the stars overhead through the skylights are akin to sleeping on the beach. Waking in the wee hours to watch the red and green lights of ships passing slowly and silently down the waterway will transport you to an unforgettable dream world.

By day Sooke Harbour House is a great place to be led around by the nose. You can't take more than a few steps anywhere on the property without running into a new and tantalizing smell. Spices and herbs abound, and not all of them are readily apparent without expert guidance. Crushing the leaf of a potted bush in the hallway reveals a fragrant edible masquerading as a decorative houseplant. With a little professional advice from the gardening staff, you can collect aromas for a bedtime game of "Herbs and Spice." Strategic application of different aromas to various parts of one's anatomy starts the game. To proceed, use the game's rule book to light the fireplace. The key to winning is to select the right fragrances to use in the right places to seduce your lover. This can be a bit tricky: Some smells will leave you salivating with desire, all right—but for turkey and stuffing, as we found out with a rosemary plant.

Day One: Evening
Dinner

Most people are captivated by the stunning view of the Strait of Juan de Fuca and the Olympic Mountain Range in Washington State. The scene is visible from just about anywhere in the bright dining area located on the ground floor of the main house. Once the initial thrill of the vista has worn off, you'll begin to notice all the artwork. Traditionally styled Coast Indian ceremonial masks and newer carvings from the younger generation of Indian artists vie for your attention with chest-high kelp candelabras and peanut-butter-colored carvings of gray whales. The owners, Sinclair and Fredrica Philip, are ardent collectors and patrons for local artists, and over the years the inn has filled with a fascinating eclectic accumulation. Let your curiosity get the better of you and ask about the origins of whatever grabs your attention.

When you finally get around to it, just reading the menu makes your mouth water: a Carpaccio of Fresh Wild Chinook Salmon Marinated in Spring Herbs, with a Salmonberry Shoot, Hop Shoot, Limpet, and Celery Root Salad, or, as an entree, Vermilion Rockfish served with a Sweet Cicely Pod, Pumpkin Seed, and Wild Sorrel Puree and a Day Lily Bud, Broccoli, and Asparagus Flavored Couscous. Or how about this: An Angel Wing Mushroom and Sweet Marjoram Sauce, decorated with a Crispy Kohlrabi and Coriander Panisse. For the curious who always wanted to know what fire-engine red tastes like, you can sample the brilliant red flowers of the honeydew melon sage. Don't be surprised to find the peppery taste of nasturtiums, the mild wintergreen of violets, or the strong citrus tang of tuberous begonias accenting your meal. For this adventure in dining you'll pay $8.00 to $15.00 for appetizers, $30.00 for entrees (a set price), and $7.00 to $9.50 for dessert (with ingredients like coriander and fennel ice cream and dried cranberry syrup).

Sooke Harbour House has one other attraction of note: A wine connoisseur washed ashore here would certainly think he or she had landed in heaven. With a thirty-five-page selection of wines and a staff who can suggest the finest choice to complement your dinner, even a novice can take pleasure in it. Although there's a fine selection of French and California wines, when in Rome . . . Some of the British Columbia wines have taken top prizes in European competitions, so if wine is your delight, linger over dinner and experiment. After all, you don't have to drive anywhere, and with the wine and fireplace to warm and soothe you, why would you want to?

DAY TWO: MORNING
Breakfast

The loser of "Herbs and Spices" has to answer the door and pour the first cup of coffee. Alternatively, unlock the door and sing out at the knock. Proper etiquette requires you not to giggle from under the covers while staff is in the room. The tasty breakfast is served in your

Munch a Bunch—of Petunias?

Many renowned restaurants have built a reputation on one signature dish and a couple of more unusual concoctions. Sooke Harbour House's celebrity comes from the chef's imaginative use of a greater range of ingredients than most restaurants have access to and the fact that the chef, the gardener, and the owners must all collaborate on each creation. The menu reflects fickle Nature, who may be stingy with certain herbs, vegetables, flowers, or fish one month and bountiful the next. The head gardener must plan months in advance to make sure the ingredients delivered are in their prime. The chef must continually meld elements one normally would not consider together to deliver a unique and tantalizing flavor. For instance, you'll only be able to sample a salad composed of wild and cultivated greens and midspring blossoms during a few weeks of the year before the menu changes to take advantage of the late-spring abundance. And who but a consummate chef would take a chance on chickpea-encrusted oysters served over arugula and hazelnut puree? (It's sensational!)

room from menu choices you leave hanging on your door the night before, along with the time you would like to see the food arrive. We suggest the full breakfast, something along the lines of an omelet with herbs and sun-dried tomatoes or pancakes with fruit and maple syrup—the menu changes daily—as you'll still receive the croissants and muffins that come with the continental breakfast. You can also have juice, cereal, yogurt, and fruit compote to round out your feast.

❧

After breakfast take a walk along **Whiffen Spit** (sounds like a bad restaurant, doesn't it?). Named for a clerk aboard one of the first European exploration ships, it's a mile-long, meandering spit of land only yards wide that juts into Sooke Bay. The parks department has created a wide gravel walkway to the end that is perfect for a brisk walk in the morning or a leisurely stroll after dinner. Seals are numerous and curious and will pace you along the entire walk. At the end you are out in the middle of the bay, closer to the opposite shore than to the Sooke Harbour House. Nature has considerately placed logs where you can relax and dream of the first Spanish sailors as they entered the strait under the shadow of the snowcapped Olympic Mountains across the way.

After your walk visit the **Blue Raven Gallery** (1971 Kaltasin Road, Sooke; 250–881–0528). To get there, drive back to Sooke Road, turn right, and go back into the town of Sooke; then turn right onto Kaltasin Road. The gallery is a showplace of the art of Victor, Edith, and Carey Newman and contains displays of carvings, prints, gold and silver jewelry, and clothing. Victor is the artist whose work adorns the room named for him at the Sooke Harbour House; Edith is a designer of wearable art, under the label Newman Ayesu Originals, and Carey, their son, is an award-winning native artist. With luck you might time your visit to coincide with the work schedule of the artists and see them as they form their creations.

DAY TWO: AFTERNOON
Lunch

Although a scrumptious light lunch, usually a seafood variation, is served in the dining room, the kitchen will pack a picnic lunch for you to take on your afternoon adventure to the **Sooke Potholes.** Take Sooke Road (the main street) left from Sooke Harbour House and through the village. About five minutes east of the town center is Sooke River Road, off to your left. There is also a sign for the Sooke Potholes before the road. Follow the road to the parking lot.

❧❧

During summer these natural pools along the Sooke River are a favorite cooling-off spot for locals, and between October and December people come for miles to watch the natural phenomenon of hundreds of salmon roiling the water as they make their way upstream to spawn. It's worth a walk up the gravel road to see the waterfall on your right at the bridge 100 yards upstream from the parking lot. You can climb to the top of the falls, but save some energy for another uphill walk that is even more spectacular.

Farther up the river, just as you begin to rise along the edge of Sooke Canyon, is a heavy metal fence stretched partly across the road. Beyond it, another ten minutes uphill, are the remains of a stupendous abandoned lodge set on the very edge of the narrow canyon. The Sooke River cascades from a rock wall into a series of waterfalls hundreds of feet below the lodge. As you round the bend, you are surprised by the unfinished skeleton of huge graying logs and stonework that leaps into view. It takes several minutes to fathom that someone built this castle out in the wilderness and then left it. We were told by several locals about the size of the abandoned château but were still speechless when we first saw it.

The lodge clings to the ledges overlooking the deepest part of the gorge. Half-completed stairs to nowhere and stone walkways built by medieval Portuguese stonemasons cantilever out into space. Abandoned rooms stare eerily at the mountains just feet from the edge. A stone fireplace, open on four sides, is so large that you can walk through it without ducking. From the waterfall below, looking up, the lodge is a mountain castle replete with broken secret stairways descending the cliffsides and a turret scratching the sky. Take care when crossing the floor covering the stone dungeons—it's easy to be absorbed in looking through the missing roof and lose your footing. Beyond the fortress the trail leads down to parapets overlooking the top of the waterfall. That there are few railings anywhere lends a delicious chill to the already moist air. Leaning out to better see the fortress, you can imagine steel being settled in the armory and an occasional neigh as creatures bed down for the night.

A caretaker lives on the premises, and with a little coaxing he might tell you the tale of a dream unfulfilled. If, as rumor has it, the project is only on hold for a few years, the next time you see it, you might have to pay several hundred dollars a night to stand next to the fireplace. Frankly, on a cloudy day we would take the forlorn mystery of the place over another high-priced retreat.

FOR MORE ROMANCE

At or near a full moon, stroll along the wide flat path of Whiffen Spit. With the moon reaching for you across the water and a light summer breeze redolent with the spice of the sea, the effect is magical. In a storm count on the sea spray as an aperitif for the double bath in your room.

ITINERARY 24
Two days and one night

MIDNIGHT IN THE GARDEN:
VICTORIA, VANCOUVER ISLAND

*V*ictoria, flower child of Canada, is a city you can visit any time of the year for a burst of spring. Many people prefer it in summer, when the weather is at its best and the city is a riot of color from hundreds of hanging flower baskets. Visit in February and not only will you beat the crowds but you can participate in the Annual Flower Count. With the sea circulating warm South Pacific currents around the city, spring comes very early here, occasionally as early as late January. Victorians, in smug celebration of winter's end, broadcast the exact number of flowers in bloom in the city on all the news channels across Canada—which endears them to their neighbors still buried in snow and ice. Stroll through the garden city on a mild February evening or nuzzle your lover for warmth on an oceanfront park bench, enjoying your early peek at the waltz of spring.

Practical notes: You'll need a car if you are going to see **Butchart Gardens** on your way into Victoria from the ferry. Guest parking is at the rear of Abigail's Hotel. Take the ferry from Tsawwassen to Swartz Bay (see the Appendix for details). If you decide to leave the car behind and take the bus, call the Gray Line (604–662–8074) for an exact bus schedule to Victoria. Buses are frequent, and the round-trip ticket is $46. You can also arrange for your Butchart Gardens tour at the same number or once you are in Victoria (250–388–5248). The three-hour tour to Butchart leaves from downtown Victoria at noon from in front of The Empress Hotel. The cost is $25 per person, including the entrance fee.

DAY ONE: MORNING

Romance at a Glance

♥ *Wander the trails of the formal Butchart Gardens (250–652–5256).*

♥ *Coddle yourself at Abigail's Hotel (250–388–5363 or 800–561–6565).*

♥ *Eat, drink, and be merry at Swans Pub and Brewery (250–361–3310).*

♥ *Kiss a butterfly at Crystal Garden (250–381–1213).*

♥ *Explore the past at the Royal British Columbia Museum (250–387–3701 or 800–661–5411).*

♥ *Take a water ferry around the inner harbor (250–480–0971).*

If you take a ferry about 10:00 A.M., you should be at **Butchart Gardens** (Box 4010, Victoria; 250–652–5256; open daily at 9:00 A.M., but phone for closing time, as it varies greatly throughout the year; $6.00 to $15.50 per person admission price, depending on time of year; two-hour minimum suggested for touring the gardens) about midday. Shortly after you leave the ferry, you'll see signs for a tourist booth (on your right). Stop and pick up a map. The trip to the gardens is about 20 km (12.5 miles), and signs mark the route to Butchart Gardens fairly well.

This fifty-acre site was formerly a worked-out quarry and was begun as a garden in 1904. The transformation to a world-class garden took years, but the results are every gardener's dream. Each month of the year has plants willing to show off their colors, from the barely curbed enthusiasm of the spring daffodils and fragrant hyacinths to the more subdued cotoneaster, holly, and pyracantha berries of the winter. Several major fountains are guaranteed to make your romantic wishes come true, and you'll delight in the formal Japanese, Italian, and Rose Gardens and perfect scenic vistas of the West Coast.

If you're traveling during the peak season of mid-June to the end of September and would like a little time and privacy to enjoy each other as you walk through the park, the staff at the garden

According to the Butchart Gardens souvenir book, the Tibetan Blue Poppy has been in the gardens since the 1920s. As the story goes, the seed for the flower was gathered by Captain Frederick Marshman Bailey, a British Army officer and spy, in the Himalayas. During a visit with Mrs. Butchart, he mentioned that he was sure there was one flower she did not possess, a Tibetan Blue Poppy. He was astounded when she showed him "his flower" in full bloom. He had passed the seeds on to the Edinburgh Botanical Garden, who in turn passed some on to Mrs. Butchart. For his discovery of the flower, Captain Bailey received the Gold Medal of the Royal Geographical Society.

suggest that you delay your trip until after the congestion eases, after 3:00 P.M. Or why not arrive even later and plan to stick around to cuddle up together on a blanket and watch the fireworks and music display? It happens every Saturday night during July and August. The display starts about fifteen minutes after dark, as late as 10:15 P.M. during early summer but around 8:30 P.M. by the end of August. The gardens are also illuminated at night and have a different, more romantic feel than during the day. Phone Butchart for all the details and exact times (250–652–5256). If you visit during the day, you can return for the night show without cost.

Don't be too concerned if your trip is in winter rather than summer. From December 1 through early January, the holiday season is celebrated in style and you won't be disappointed by the array of lights and decorations.

DAY ONE: AFTERNOON
Lunch

There are several restaurants at Butchart Gardens (main number 250–652–5256) to choose from when hunger pangs strike. History buffs may want to opt for **The Dining Room Restaurant,** in the original Butchart residence. For $8 to $12, the restaurant serves a variety of salads, soups, vegetarian quiches, seafood pastas, and (you're on the West Coast) salmon. Or go more casual with the **Blue Poppy Restaurant** or head for the **Quarry Coffeehouse** or the **Soda Fountain** for pastries and beverages. The map you get on arrival will direct you to the choices. As another alternative, take along a picnic. Once you leave the main highway toward Butchart, stop in and grab some fixings at one of the stores along the way. Places are set up for picnickers within Butchart Gardens.

๑๑๐

Back on the road, follow the signs to Highway 17 into Victoria. The highway will eventually turn into Blanchard Street, one of the main streets in downtown Victoria. Once in the downtown core, turn left onto Burdett Avenue and follow it for 2 blocks to Vancouver Street, where you turn right. Go along to McClure and turn right to find your home for the night.

Abigail's Hotel (906 McClure Street, Victoria; 250–388–5363 or 800–561–6565; $145 to $289 with breakfast, phone about winter rates; Romance Packages available) started life in the 1930s as an apartment building. Ten years ago it was successfully converted into a sixteen-room European-style hotel. It's well located, at only 3 blocks to the ocean, the downtown area, and Beacon Hill Park. The warm appeal of the entrance lobby will be endorsed by the welcome given to you by the innkeepers, Frauke and Daniel Behune.

Ask for the Foxglove Room, with a queen-size, four-poster canopy bed smothered in a goose down duvet. The double Jacuzzi tub is just the place for a double scrub before settling onto the leather love seat conveniently positioned in front of the crackling fire. And the best news is that exercise is built in: The Foxglove Room is on the second floor, and there's no elevator. What better justification for a nap or a relaxing soak for two in the tub?

A short, ten-minute walk down Quadra Street from Abigail's is **Beacon Hill Park.** This seventy-five-acre park, dating from 1889, has everything from formal gardens and fountains to peacocks and swans in ponds—and, during spring and summer, flowers of every description. Some of the Garry oaks in the park are 350-plus years old. During summer, concerts, variety shows, and other entertainment go on in the band shell. Something usually happens on Sunday, and a complete schedule is available from the Tourist Information Booth in front of The Empress hotel.

For those of you who would rather see more gardens, call **Victorian Garden Tours** (250–721–2797; $29 per person). Its staff will take you on a tour to see some of the other fabulous gardens in the area, including the Hatley Park Garden at Royal Rhodes University, with its formal Italian garden, Japanese garden, and rose collection; Saxe Point Park, with plants that do not grow anywhere else in Canada; and several other gardens of note.

After wandering hither and yon, you may well be ready for a glass of sherry and appetizers. Both are served between 5:00 and 7:00 P.M. in the book-lined library at Abigail's. Just sink into one of the overstuffed chairs and put your feet up. Or what about a bubble bath? The tub is made for two, and the small shop in the lobby sells candles so that you can set the scene with faint flickering light.

DAY ONE: EVENING

Swans Pub and Brewery (506 Pandora Avenue, at the corner of Wharf Street; 250–361–3310) is part of a complex that includes a fine-dining restaurant, a superb pub, a hotel, a microbrewery, and a jazz club. Located in Olde Towne across from the inner harbor, it's easily recognizable in summer by the multitude of flowers adorning this heritage building. Although the pub's interior is one of the better pub decors we've seen, with lots of polished light woods, brick, and brass, the best place to sit to people-watch is in the glassed-in patio under the flowers. If you enjoy beer and want to try something different, order the Arctic Ale, a mild light beer, or, for abundant flavor, the Olde Towne Bavarian Lager, aged for six weeks before serving. This drinking establishment has been voted Victoria's Best Pub and no wonder. Under the pub is one of British Columbia's few microbreweries, **Buckerfields Brewery** (800–668–7926 or 250–361–3310), and beers and ales are hand-pumped to the pub above. Free brewery tours are held at 2:00 P.M. Monday through Friday, so if you're nearby shopping, mark this on your list of things to stop by and see (sip).

Part of what you'll enjoy most are the paintings and sculptures hanging or standing throughout the hotel, pub, and restaurant; these constitute one of the largest private collections of art in Canada. From portraits to the abstract, there is something to fascinate everyone. One of the official portraits done for but rejected by Pierre Elliot Trudeau, perhaps Canada's most famous prime minister, hangs in the restaurant. The whole complex is extremely well done and attracts a lively crowd at all hours.

Dinner

You can walk through the pub into the **Fowl and Fish Café and Oyster House** (beside Swans Pub and hotel; 800–668–7926; $10 to $17) or enter from the street. The menu has some old favorites like wild boar, ostrich, and emu, as well as the run-of-the-coop items like chicken. As you might expect with such exotic birds on the menu, the most popular dish according to the staff, is the prime rib. The less adventurous can munch their way through an assortment of more traditional dishes like seafood and pastas. For an appetizer try the nut-breaded Brie or the crab cakes.

ᏋᎥᎦ

After dinner scoot downstairs to the **Millennium Jazz Club** (1601 Store Street, under the Oyster House; 250–360–9098; open 7:00 P.M. to 2:00 A.M. Thursday through Saturday and 7:00 P.M. to midnight Sunday; cover charge ranges between $3.00 and $5.00 and on Sunday there's a dinner-dance combo for $12, closed the rest of the week). You can sway the night away with live jazz bands playing permutations like Afro-Cuban, Afro-Brazilian, and salsa to fill the dance floor.

DAY TWO: MORNING

Breakfast

Breakfast is served between 8:00 and 9:30 A.M. in the dining room just inside the front door. This four-course gourmet breakfast will attack your willpower with hot homemade muffins and scones, followed by a choice of main dishes. These might include poached eggs for the savory option, apple strudel for the sweet, and vegetable pie for the heart-smart selection. It would be nice to have the heart-smart selection, if only the strudel didn't have your name on it. . . .

For extra decadence you can arrange to have your breakfast in your room. It'll arrive at your door in a large wicker basket with champagne and orange juice. Of course, if you do, you'll miss the butterfly kisses at the next stop. Well, maybe not.

◦✦◦

Crystal Garden (700 block of Douglas Street; 250–381–1213; open 10:00 A.M. to 4:00 P.M. daily, $7.00) is a promenade over walkways and bridges through a jungle of greenery and color where you can walk hand in hand, rain or shine. This glass-roofed building is home to more than sixty-five species of endangered exotic birds and animals in a mass of hundreds of tropical plants and blooms. Every inhabitant you see here, except the humans, are either already on the International Endangered Species List or soon will be. Crystal Garden is very involved in breeding and conservation programs. Be sure to see the world's smallest monkeys, which are only 4 inches high when fully grown. In the Butterfly Room stand very still and wait for one of the hundreds of butterflies to discover you. Bright colors seem to attract them, and with the right kind of lipstick, you might have the thrill of actually kissing a butterfly!

The glass hall was opened in 1925 and once housed one of the largest indoor swimming pools in the British Empire. Imagine splashing around in there!

Come out and saunter down to the harbor, just across from The Empress hotel, for a forty-five minute tour by small passenger ferry with **Victoria Harbour Ferry Company**

(9922 Old Esquimalt, Victoria; 250–480–0971; summer hours 10:00 A.M. to 10:00 P.M. and winter hours posted at the ferry stops). You can get on and off the ferry during stops at marinas and hotels en route. The ferries follow a schedule, so you just get on another one when you're ready to travel on. The Harbour Tour costs $10.

DAY TWO: AFTERNOON
Lunch

For some of the best fish-and-chips to be eaten this side of the Atlantic, go to **Barb's Place** (310 St. Lawrence, Victoria; 250–384–6515; $8.00 for a huge portion), at Fisherman's Wharf. It's not the heavy-grease variety you so often find. You can walk to Fisherman's Wharf, but a better idea is to stop en route of your Harbor Tour by ferry. One order of two pieces of halibut or codfish is large enough for two. Barb's is a Victoria institution and is known around the world. In conversations with other travelers, Barb's gets mentioned right after The Empress when the talk turns to Victoria.

☙❦❧

Just up from the ferry dropoff is the home of the **Royal British Columbia Museum** (675 Belleville Street, Victoria; 250–387–3701 or 800–661–5411, open daily except Christmas and New Year's Day, 9:00 A.M. to 5:00 P.M. and until 6:00 P.M. in July and August; $5.35). The museum, founded in 1886, is known worldwide as a center for research and museum innovation. Even if you don't consider yourself a museum person, try this one. The museum is highly creative in its approach. Rather than endless displays of items, you'll wander along the streets of the British Columbia of the past. In the Modern History Gallery, for instance, you'll become part of the romance of the West as you enter an old rail station that looks like it's ready to receive passengers out here on the frontier. Or climbing the stairs to the Grand Hotel, you'll find yourself immersed in a completely decorated room for rent. As you walk along, you'll discover little nooks and alleys holding authentic representations of old Chinatown, a chemist's shop, and a smithy.

The Natural History Gallery and the First Peoples Gallery are just as realistic and draw you into their stories rather than walking along beside displays. In one area of the museum are life-size replicas of various sea mammals that you would swear move. (Better for us to take away the surprise than for you to have a heart attack when you round the corner and run into the sea lion.) One of the best displays is on the outside of the museum, near the front. Totems and mortuary poles have been collected for the museum and arranged under cover at the front of the building. If you look closely at the black-and-white and sepia pictures with each display, you'll be floored to realize some of these poles were in use until about fifty years ago, just about the time Elvis was getting his start.

By the time you finish with the museum, you'll realize how close history really is here. This was the frontier until just a few years ago, and there are still people living in Victoria who remember much of what the museum has on display. For example, one gentleman had a disagreement with a grizzly while working his trap line and managed to survive only by jamming his arm far into the bear's mouth, so the animal couldn't chew on his head anymore. Despite horrid injuries, the man walked and snow-sledded for days to safety. There are a hundred stories of fights for survival with the mountains and the sea. When you go through the displays, remember that some of these mountain men and women are still living in Victoria and the frontier spirit is still here.

FOR MORE ROMANCE

Prince of Whales (ticket office is across from The Empress hotel, directly under the Visitor Information Centre; 250–383–4884; open year-round; $65 for an inflatable ride and $70 for a covered boat) is a good outfit to contact during whale-watching season (March to mid-October). The organization offers several departures per day, claims a success rate of more than 90 percent and can take you out in zodiac boats or all-weather boats.

The **Beach at Cattle Point** is the beach of choice for sunbathers. The view across the Strait of Juan de Fuca to the Olympic Mountain Range is breathtaking.

ITINERARY 25
Two days and one night

CASTLE IN THE MOUNTAINS:
MALAHAT, VANCOUVER ISLAND

*T*here's a reason that mystics through the ages have chosen mountaintops to grasp heaven. The God's-eye view of the countryside literally makes everyday cares look smaller, and shouts for your attention from the valley below reach you only faintly. The air is crisper and cleaner, and colors are brighter. Your vision is clear.

Once upon an ancient time (and very far away), teachers ushered the novice into the mysteries with lessons of sensuality. The distractions of the body were to be not rejected as a clamor to be quelled but channeled as a path to enlightenment. Their prescription for immortality accented a relaxed frame of mind, constant and careful attention to the body's messages, and scrupulous cleanliness through bathing. Food could be not gulped but slowly savored. Companions were honored for the heavenly ecstasy they could thrill you to.

Years practicing Tantric Yoga and an affinity for the Kama Sutra as a bedside companion would guide the new initiate. With a lifetime of introspection and some outside help, the acolyte might see heaven.

There is another way.

Practical notes: You can pamper body and soul with this itinerary at any time of the year, but the salmon run is at its peak during October and November. The drive is particularly appealing in fall, when the leaves are changing color. Toss your swimming gear in your overnight case, along with something decent to wear for dinner. While there isn't a dress code, most patrons do tend to dress up a bit. For general information about the area, contact **Tourism Vancouver Island,** 302–45 Bastion Square, Victoria, BC V8W 1J1; 250–382–3551). You'll be leaving from Tsawwassen Ferry Terminal to catch the ferry to Swartz Bay on Vancouver Island, so check the Appendix for information. This itinerary combines easily with those for Victoria, Sooke, or the Wickanninish on the West Coast of Vancouver Island.

DAY ONE: LATE MORNING/EARLY AFTERNOON

Ferries leave frequently for Vancouver Island. If you catch one about 11:00 A.M., you'll be on the island about 12:30 P.M., in time to explore a little before arriving at the resort for your late-afternoon spa appointments.

Romance at a Glance

♥ *Baby yourself at The Aerie Resort (250–743–7115).*

♥ *Dine at the restaurant at the Aerie.*

♥ *Relax with a full-body massage.*

♥ *Stop at Goldstream Provincial Park.*

Lunch

We always consider the ferry ride as part of our time away; it lulls us into a more relaxed frame of mind before we reach the island. Though every large ferry in the fleet has at least one cafeteria-style restaurant where you can find something palatable to eat, our favorite place to lunch aboard is the Pacific Buffet on the *Spirit of Vancouver Island* and the *Spirit of British Columbia.* Both ships have a special dining room with a 180-degree view. Starting at 11:00 A.M. they have an all-you-can-eat hot and cold buffet brunch for $11.95. Sit next to the windows for the best view. After eating stroll hand in hand around the deck and enjoy the fresh salt air. The scenery is outstanding, and you'll have a chance to do some serious people- and bird-watching.

෯෯

When you drive off the ferry, continue along Highway 17 toward Victoria for approximately twenty minutes. (You'll see the Tourist Information Bureau on your right a few kilometers from the ferry exit. Stop in for a map.) Next watch for a major interchange with **Highway 1—Up-Island Trans Canada** and follow it north away from Victoria for approximately twenty-five minutes to reach the scenic **Malahat Drive.** It's a winding road, with lots of maple, western red cedar, and Douglas firs hugging the freeway.

Stop en route for a visit to **Goldstream Provincial Park.** In the parking lot and throughout the preserve are enormous red cedar trees; the largest and oldest are 450 to 500 years old. Take the time to get out of your car and walk around on some of the walking trails through the cedars and along Goldstream Creek. This is true rainforest, and the soft, spongy moss covering every surface and hanging from the trees creates a sublime green velvet painting.

The Goldstream Visitor's Centre (250–478–9414) is worth the short, ten-minute stroll from the parking lot. As you emerge from the woods, you're at the head of a marsh where Goldstream Creek enters Saanich Inlet. Arrive during the salmon spawning season and hundreds of bald eagles lining the marsh will give you a onceover before returning to fishing. They congregate annually to gorge on the salmon in October and November. At the peak of the salmon season, during the second or third week of November, when the river is completely full, 20,000 to 30,000 Chinook, chum, and coho salmon are moving up the creek. Up to 60,000 reach the river each year. You have only to watch for a few moments to see an eagle arrow from its perch and snatch a prize from the water. Occasionally, one is overmatched by a fish, and for a few moments you may witness a primeval struggle as the salmon refuses to be lifted and the eagle will not be denied. The boardwalk trails along the marsh edge will give you a front-row seat.

With luck you'll also be at the center when the art exhibition is going on. The exhibition takes place every second year, displaying the creations of Vancouver and Vancouver Island artists whose specialty is nature-centered artwork. Some of these works are serious investments of time and artistic talent and capture the spirit of the Pacific Coast with panache.

When you're back in your car, drive about 2 kilometers north (take a right out of the visitor's center along Malahat Drive) to the peak of the hill to a pullover spot for a panoramic view of Saanich Inlet. Later watch for signs to **Spectacle Lake,** and turn left off the highway. Drive about 0.5 kilometer and turn right at the sign for **The Aerie Resort** (P.O. Box 108, Malahat; 250–743–7115; $150 to $395 includes full breakfast; Romance Packages feature two nights' accommodations, breakfast each morning, a seven-course dinner on one night, a bottle of sparkling wine, a large fruit basket, and a dozen red roses, for $575 to $900, depending on the room and the season). Drive to the end of the road and prepare yourself for a bit of a shock. Unexpectedly, there among the dark towering trees is a multilevel, Mediterranean-style building that would stand out anywhere. Here in the midst of forest, it is almost dreamlike. The light cream of the walls, combined with the red-tile roof and turquoise awnings, is very dramatic against the dark green backdrop of the woods.

The Aerie Resort was built as a secluded retreat where one could be pampered and hidden from the rest of the world. As you enter the door to the resort, clear your mind of the mundane aspects of day-to-day life. You're here to be pampered and coddled. Concentrate only on the physical and sensual pleasures. An uncluttered mind makes Nirvana easier to achieve.

The Aerie offers a variety of rooms and suites, but go for the Raven Room if you can. Located in the Residence, separate from the main building, it's also the home of the spa. The Raven Room is 1,000 square feet of decadent luxury. In the sitting area are a sofa and a reclining chair grouped around a Persian carpet. The wide balcony outside has a couple of deck chairs and a view of the inlet, the mountains, and a peaceful garden with a pond and soothing waterfall: restful enough to make you not want to move. Between the sleeping area and the sitting area is the gas fireplace, positioned to be enjoyed from either section of the

This "Castle in the Mountains," as the owners refer to it, is the dream child of Austrian natives Leo and Maria Schuster. During a visit to Vancouver Island, they knew they had found their dream home when they first set foot on the land. The way the resort is situated high above the Malahat gives an unparalleled view of the islands, the fjord of Finlayson Arm, and the Olympic Mountains.

suite. And just waiting for you, in front of the window in the sleeping area, is a double soaker tub. Beyond that, displayed against the wall and looking out toward the wonderful mountainscape, is a king-size leather sled bed. Imagine yourself sinking into the warm folds of soft Christian Dior linens and a fluffy down duvet. Ah, bliss. But not just yet.

Call the spa, **Aesthetically Yours** (250–743–3777; $45 to $340 for treatments lasting up to three hours) at the same time as you reserve your room. Staff can tell you about the services they offer. We suggest that your first choice be a double massage ($345 for a couple for the full treatment), with the two of you in adjoining rooms. While one of you is receiving a full-body massage to ease the tense muscles of your back and shoulders, your partner is having extensive foot and calf treatment with a reflexology foot massage. Gently scented creams are slowly massaged in while you lie in a darkened room listening to the soft music of babbling brooks or rustling trees. Your muscles loosen under the gentle kneading, and tension drains away. Halfway through your time the masseuses will change places and give each of you the other treatment. The wonderful part of a dual massage is that you won't have to worry about your partner having excess energy afterward. You'll both be mellow bundles wrapped up in your robes, with just enough energy to light the fire or run the water in preparation for a soak in the deep double tub when you pad back to your room. If you time it right, you'll have just enough time for the restful nap the sled bed promises.

DAY ONE: EVENING

Dinner

The short stroll over to the main hotel is a pleasure, with the music of the fountains and the scent of the trees and flowers to accompany you. Don't worry about the rain—plenty of umbrellas are at each of the doors to the resort. Just pick one up, use it, and leave it at your destination. Even if the food were dismal, which it most assuredly is not, dining at the hotel restaurant (entrees $28 to $34, or the set seven-course meal at $60 per person) would be an experience. The dining room is mostly glass, which makes for panoramic views of the fjord and Olympic Mountains throughout. But ask for a window seat anyway, unless the weather is good enough to sit outside on the balcony. Try to time your dinner so you are seated just before sunset.

High-backed chairs and crisp linen-covered tables with silver and delicate glass are all gently lit by the soft light of many candles. Linger over dinner. This is West Coast cuisine at its finest, with a French touch to accent the experience. The dishes are a delight to your senses and deserve the time to be savored. Hold hands, sip a fine wine, and talk only of good and pleasing subjects. Absorb the easy music of the pianist. If you have favorites, the musician will be more than happy to play them for you.

❀

After dinner wander back to your room to change into your swimming gear and stroll over to the pool for a dip. The walls of the rooftop indoor pool are almost entirely glass and thus appear to bring the outdoors inside. There is also plenty of room surrounding the pool for ferns and lounging furniture, which makes it a lovely place to paddle by night or day. If the soak you had earlier in your tub wasn't enough, an outdoor hot tub lets you sit back and watch the stars.

DAY TWO: MORNING

Breakfast

Another sensuous experience awaits you at breakfast—definitely a meal to idle over. Along with croissants and muffins and a choice of cereals comes a hot dish that could be Sockeye Salmon Eggs Benedict with Hollandaise; Potato Hash with Venison and Maple Sausage; Rhubarb and Cranberry Chutney, Poached Eggs, and Chive Creme Fraiche; or Lemon Buttermilk Griddle Cakes with Fresh Strawberries, Citrus Curd, and Whipped Cream. It's going to make your toast and coffee next week look pretty shabby!

Don't rush; you've nothing that has to be done. The morning meal is served in the dining room. If the room looked intimate and romantic in the fading light last night, in the daylight it is breathtakingly expansive. The light colors of the walls and furnishings give the room an airy feeling that's even more apparent in full daylight.

※

After breakfast the options are yours. Another spa treatment? You'll find a wide range to choose from. Aromatherapy, maybe. Or another few laps in the pool? Spectacle Lake is only a few minutes away and has a trail perfect for a leisurely walk. The tennis courts also await you. But perhaps the deck off your room is calling your name, and it's your time to watch the world pass you by.

FOR MORE ROMANCE

For an even faster start to your spoiling, skip the car and the ferry and fly in by helicopter. The resort has a helipad for quick escapes. For those who need extra activity, golfing, sailing, chartered fishing, hiking, and horseback riding are all available close by. Just ask the front-desk staff.

FERRY TALES

ITINERARY 26
Two days and one night

CREATIVE JUICES:
SALT SPRING ISLAND

*M*ore than a day on Salt Spring Island and you can't help having the impression that Vincent van Gogh would be right at home living here in a teepee, selling his paintings at the Saturday craft fair and swilling beer with his friend Paul Gauguin. Especially when a mist rolls in off the strait and blurs the sharp contours of the mountains or the sun spills bright colors across the countryside, you can smell the creative juices pitching up yet another awe-inspiring painting somewhere on the island.

Salt Spring probably has more painters, sculptors, authors, and accomplished craftspeople than all the art schools of the province combined. What they need to consummate their dance of creativity is you as an appreciative audience. In turn, if watching creative genius at work is an aphrodisiac for the two of you, this visit promises to be remarkably seductive. Indulge each other's passion . . . for the arts. The artists of Salt Spring beckon . . .

Practical notes: Summer is the most popular time to visit Salt Spring Island, and you'll find fewer closures of galleries and studios. For general tourist information about the area, contact the **Salt Spring Chamber of Commerce** (121 Lower Ganges Road, Salt Spring Island, BC, V8K 2T1; 250–537–5252; fax: 250–537–4276). For a small fee (approximately $5.00), the organization will send you a host of information on the island.

DAY ONE: LATE MORNING/EARLY AFTERNOON

Disembark from the ferry and follow the crowd along Long Harbour Road until you reach the T in the road. Turn left onto Upper Ganges Road and left again on Lower Ganges Road. A short hop and you're in **Ganges.**

If you didn't have Salt Spring Island information sent to you, your first stop should be at the Tourist Information Centre in the village. You'll see the signs for TOURIST INFORMATION on the left-hand side, at 121 Lower Ganges Road. More studios and galleries are outside the village than in Ganges, and the **Studio Tour** map provided by the helpful tourist-information people lists thirty-two locations you can visit. On the reverse side of the map are listings of contact information, hours of operation, and types of studios—whether an artist is a painter, a weaver, or a potter, for example. Your particular interests will dictate the route you'll want to follow. Contact the artists before you journey out to see them, to be sure their studios are open. Or just explore and take your chances.

Romance at a Glance

♥ *Let Anne's Oceanfront Hideaway spoil you (250–537–0851).*

♥ *Tempt your pocketbook with tours of art studios.*

♥ *Dine at the Seacourt Restaurant (250–537–4611).*

♥ *Sup on soup at the Alfresco Waterfront Restaurant and Café (250–537–5979).*

The stores in Ganges village are worth a look too. A surprising absence of kitsch exists probably because there are so many artists on the island that store owners are embarrassed to display the normal tourist-trap regalia. Several galleries—such as the **Naikai Gallery** (in the gray-blue Grace Point Square complex) and the **Pegasus Gallery** (Mouats Lower Mall)—carry West Coast artists' work (e.g., work by Carol Evans and Carol Haigh). Along the waterfront **Jill Louise Campbell** has her own gallery, which is worth a look, and the **Clay Works** (Mouats Lower Mall) features unusual hand-formed clay. Reflecting the eclectic island tone are shops catering to the collector, such as

From Vancouver on the mainland, you'll be taking the ferry from the Tsawwassen Ferry Terminal to Long Harbour on Salt Spring Island. (See the Appendix for more information.) But this itinerary also dovetails neatly with any of those to Vancouver Island. The twenty-minute ferry ride from Crofton on Vancouver Island (approximately one hour north along the Island Highway from Victoria) will transport you to Vesuvius on Salt Spring Island. Once at Vesuvius, you are very close to Anne's Oceanfront Hideaway. When your stay is over, you can ferry from Long Harbour, near the town of Ganges, back to Tsawwassen on the mainland. You can also easily combine this itinerary with any of the other Gulf Island itineraries.

The **Stone Walrus** (122 Lower Ganges Road; 250–537–9896), which brings together artists from all over the globe.

To get to **Anne's Oceanfront Hideaway** (168 Simson Road, Salt Spring Island, BC V8K 1E2; 250–537–0851; fax: 250–537–0861; $135 to $200, including breakfast), travel back out Lower Ganges Road the way you came in but past Upper Ganges Road to Vesuvius Bay Road. After driving about 7.5 kilometers (4 miles), you should be watching for Sunset Drive, turning off to your right. If you end up at Vesuvius Harbour, you've gone too far and should turn back about 500 meters for the turnoff.

Sunset Drive winds and twists through the forest. Stay on it until the road veers slightly to the right. There, off to the left, is Simson Road. Turn left onto Simson and watch for the carved sign on your right. Turn right, up the driveway, and park your car.

Ruth-Anne and Rick Broad have done a wonderful job of creating a warm environment for their guests. From the welcoming smiles and fragrant cookies, you'll feel you've come to the right place. The top floor of this new house is given over to four guest rooms that have been individually decorated, each with two recliner wingback chairs, down duvets, percale sheets, and sleep-inducing beds and all with ocean views. You're welcome to enter through the front door of the house, but there's also a separate entrance to the second floor, with a staircase from the outside. One of the rooms is wheelchair accessible, and there is an elevator.

Though all the rooms are a delight, the Garry Oak is definitely the special-occasion suite, with its high-off-the-floor, four-poster bed, its gas fireplace and, oh, that soaker tub. The tub is surrounded by mirrors on three sides and is right in the main room. Dim the lights and turn on the fireplace: bliss.

The room is set for romance, right down to the pretty little heart-shaped doily under the water glasses.

DAY ONE: EVENING
Dinner

The **Seacourt Restaurant** (149 Fulford Ganges Road, Suite 108, Ganges; 250–537–4611; $12 to $23) is an excellent choice for dinner. It's on the waterfront in Ganges and features a varied menu, including a selection of Thai dishes. A delicious choice is the Ginger Pork Medallions, made with white wine and crystallized ginger. Some of the house special-ties, such as the seafood Creole and peppercorn veal, are prepared at your tableside. Sit back and enjoy the aromas and watch the busy marina.

☙❧

After dinner head back to Anne's. Sit out on the wraparound veranda or stroll down to the waterfront to take a paddle in the canoe. If the evening is cool, spend time in the living room or study reading, talking, or simply gazing at one another. Of course, the warm water of the hot tub breaking over your bodies may call to you loudest of all. You'll even have an ocean view while you splash around.

Later fill the tub with warm soapy water, dim the lights, turn on the fireplace, and turn out all the other lights to set the mood. Afterward pull on your cozy bathrobes and slippers, grab your bottle of wine with two goblets, and sit out on your deck to watch the boat lights making their way up the channel.

DAY TWO: MORNING

It's possible to lie in bed all morning, drinking tea and admiring the mountains and the sea from your clifftop hideaway, but artists are depending on you to help shape their world, are waiting for you to give them sustenance (if not in cash, then at least in praise).

Morning tea and coffee will arrive outside your door on a rolling tea trolley that you wheel into your room. Pull the trolley up by your reclining chair and sip your beverage by the fireplace or take it out on the deck to enjoy the ocean view—or lounge in bed, if you'd rather laze a bit. This is the time to try out the double shower with dual controls. . . . just don't forget the breakfast waiting for you downstairs.

Breakfast

Breakfast is served with the other guests in the dining room or on the veranda looking out over Houston Passage and the mountains of Vancouver Island. This is not a meal to be hurried, so allow time for it. Sip your juice, and toast your loved one.

Breakfast is a taste experience. The menu changes, of course, but you can expect some yummy baked goods to come from the kitchen—maybe blueberry muffins or spice buns. Rick also has a recipe for some hearty multigrain bread that he developed himself and cooks up in his breadmaker; smear it with Saskatoon berry jam. Along with fresh seasonal fruit, you'll get a hot dish, perhaps Egg Blossoms—a baked egg done in phyllo pastry in the shape of a blossom—and lamb patty with an English chutney of apples, dates, and carrots. Don't be concerned if you have a food allergy as Rick and Ruth-Anne will be happy to work around it. Just let them know when you make your reservations.

❦

Fortified, either continue on your studio tour, or, if you missed some of Ganges, visit the other shops and galleries awaiting you in the village.

Lunch

Hungry? Bet you thought it would never happen after the large breakfast. Fortunately, Ganges offers numerous places to eat. Our choice for lunch is definitely the **Alfresco Waterfront Restaurant and Café** (3106–115 Fulford Ganges Road; 250–537–5979; $6.00 to $9.00). It's tucked down on the waterfront behind the main road where you visited the Tourist Information Centre, to the left of the gray-blue Grace Point Square complex (here's when your Ganges map is going to be invaluable).

Though the restaurant offers a fair selection of tasty treats, soup lovers will be especially delighted. Five or six kinds of soup are prepared every day, such as cream of cauliflower, smoked chicken and black bean, garlic sausage, and broccoli basil cream. If you can't choose between them, it's not a problem, for the menu has samplers of two or three different kinds. If each of you takes a different sampler, you'll end up testing the whole lot. No, so far the chef is not selling the recipes, although staff are asked often.

❦

After lunch take the short walk that begins in front of the Alfresco Waterfront Restaurant and Café and meanders along Grace Point for a short distance along the shore in front of the condominium complex.

FOR MORE ROMANCE

Rent a scooter from **Heritage Car and Truck Rental** (161 Lower Ganges Road; 250–537–4225; fax: 250–537–4322; open May to November; $30 for four hours and $50 for

With their art, the creative craftspeople of the island will nourish you with tidbits of excitement sifted from your unconscious. They intend to disarm you, force logic from your head, teach you about surrender. Once past the scimitars of your opinions to your sweet and wise center, they can tease out inspired self-discovery to be shared later with your lover over a golden glass of wine or a dimly lit pillow. As a catalyst for seduction, nothing surpasses the sensuous curve of a sculptor's creation, the rough textures and seared clay of the potter's wheel, or the mellow chiaroscuro of a child's face peering from a painting.

twenty-four hours) and tool around the island that way. Staff can pick you up and drop you off at the ferry for free if you want to leave your car behind on the other side.

Take the **Salt Spring Nursery Tour.** You can get a map listing the locations throughout the island, along with actual addresses and telephone numbers, from the Tourist Information Centre in Ganges. Five nurseries are listed on the tour, spread from one end of the island to the other. They are not open year-round, so it's important to check the times before going.

ITINERARY 27
Two days and one night

SNUGGLING IN SNUG COVE:
BOWEN ISLAND

Bowen Island is a morsel in the mouth of the fjord of Howe Sound. It's a lifetime away from the big city, a place where people don't often worry about locking up their belongings and residents give you only a four-digit phone number, because everyone on the island has the same first three numbers. Rural roads squeeze into one lane to get around big trees, and mighty battles rage about expansion. Country cottages cozy up to the pillared monstrosities of the rich, all with the same splendid peekaboo views of Howe Sound or the nearby islands. Suntanned arbutus trees rustle in the wind down by the shore, while grapes sweeten in a sheltered microvalley. This island sports a mini-mall (Artisans Lane) with what has to be the most spectacular view of mountains and sea from any mall in North America. The island has long been a favorite getaway for Vancouverites because it's so close to the city. A trip to Bowen is a short, forty-five-minute drive from downtown, including a scenic, twenty-minute ferry ride from Horseshoe Bay.

Practical notes: Fall is a wonderful time to visit Bowen Island, for not only are most of the tourists gone but the lack of leaves on the trees can mean much better views. Contact the **Bowen Island Chamber of Commerce** (RR 1, Box 199, Bowen Island, BC, V0N 1G0) for information, maps, and the like concerning the island. Failing that, you can get information from most of the shopkeepers in Snug Cove once you reach the island. Pack a set of clothes suitable for horseback riding. The Horseshoe Bay Ferry Terminal is your departure point for this trip (see the Appendix).

Romance at a Glance

♥ *Munch a lunch from the Breakfast Café while hiking (604–947–0550).*

♥ *Have a pale ale at Doc Morgan's (604–947–0808.*

♥ *Relax your weary body at the Vineyard at Bowen Island (604–947–0028 or 800–718–9463).*

♥ *Dine in style at the Beggar's Purse Restaurant (604–947–0550).*

♥ *Ride the countryside on a Norwegian Fjord horse from Evergreen Acres (604–947–2982).*

DAY ONE: LATE MORNING/EARLY AFTERNOON

The ferry service between the mainland and the aptly named **Snug Cove** is frequent, but if you have a schedule to keep, check the ferry timetable before you go (888–223–3779). If you arrive early for the ferry, check your car in and then wander and shop along the boardwalk within view of the wharf, or just admire the spectacular view of the mountains and Howe Sound until the ship pulls into Horseshoe Bay. You'll have time to get back to your car while the ferry docks and unloads.

Lunch

Snug Cove is very small, and you can't get lost. Park your car anywhere you can find a place on the road or in the parking lot to your left just after you exit the ferry, so you can stroll around. We like to time our arrival on Bowen to allow a visit to **The Breakfast Café** (Orchard Square, Snug Cove; 604–947–0550) before it closes for the day at 1:00 P.M. The restaurant is housed upstairs—the lower level is a fresh produce market—in one of the early (1920s) buildings in Snug Cove. The menu is primarily breakfast fare: waffles dripping in syrup or fresh fruit and a variety of smoothie drinks that will slide down your throat and possibly add a few quality calories to your frame. Check the chalkboard for the sandwich specials, such as eggplant on focaccia bread with a tangy vinaigrette sauce. The sandwiches are worth eating even if you've already had lunch. Ask for your sandwich to go and you're all set for an impromptu picnic. Now, don't leave without having a good look around at the decor, as the next time you see it, it will look completely different: the Breakfast Café by day; the Beggar's Purse Restaurant by night.

If you need something a little sweet to round out your meal or picnic, meander along Government Street and drop in at **The Oven Door Bakery** for a pastry. With lunch safely taken care of, begin your wanderings around Snug Cove. **Cookoons & Company** in the Seabreeze Building (604–947–2324) has gift items, candles, kitchen knickknacks, cards, and the like to tempt your wallet. Next door is **Books on Bowen** (604–947–2929), a bookstore with a great selection of books written by authors who reside on the island. The **Plum Tree** and **Vonigo** (604–947–0299) have, well, everything: artwork, pottery, and collectibles of all sorts.

After you've exhausted the shops, stroll along the boardwalk, cross the bridge, and amble through the park to the entrance for the walk up **Dorman Point Trail** (about 4 kilometers round-trip). While not a tough hike, it does get rather steep in places. At the top there are plenty of huge, partly moss-covered, and relatively flat rocks to spread out both yourselves and your repast. The view is toward Vancouver, which is mostly hidden, and out over the Strait of Georgia. The water traffic is fairly heavy here, ranging from tankers moving up to the multi-billion-dollar log mills at the port of Squamish at the head of the sound to Chinese junks. All the ferries from Departure Bay on Vancouver Island cross through the passage between where you are sitting and Horseshoe Bay, hidden directly across from you.

In late afternoon drop by the upstairs pub at **Doc Morgan's** (604–947–0808), back in Snug Cove, for a Bowen Island beer. If the weather is fine, you can sit on the deck and watch the sunset turn the mountains of Howe Sound gold and purple out over the marina. As an extra treat during midweek, smugly toast the island's rush hour (around 5:30 P.M.) as a flood of suited commuters exits the ferry from Vancouver. Don't blink or you'll miss the only scurrying that happens on the island.

The road that comes off the ferry turns into Grafton Road, which takes you to **The Vineyard at Bowen Island** (687 Cates Lane, Bowen Island; 604–947–0028 or 800–718–9463; $140 to $180). Drive up the road for about five minutes before taking a left turn onto Cates Hill Road. Just before the turn you'll notice a big blue sign announcing a B&B with a left arrow. After the turn, within meters you'll see a sign on your left. Turn onto the lane and roll down your window to release the button to automatically open the gate. The gate is not to keep out two-legged strangers but to control the deer, whose greatest delight in life is to devour every grape your hosts have so painstakingly planted. As you make your way along the winding drive to the guest house, the vineyards will appear on your left, with the mountains towering in the background. On the right is your home for the night.

Elena and Lary Waldman built the Vineyard at Bowen Island, which opened in 1995 and has proved to be very popular. Weekend visits need to be booked three to four weeks in advance. Never hesitate to call about availability, though, as the innkeepers may have had a cancellation. Each guest room has its own private entrance and a view of the vineyard and mountains. All the rooms are decorated with original artwork—much of it by local artists—and other treasures the owners have collected over the years. The Deluxe Rooms on the ground floor are the same in layout, but be sure to ask for one bed, as some are outfitted with doubles. There's a fireplace to warm your toes in each room, but if you want a soaker tub, request one of the Luxury Suites on the second floor. And be sure to leave time for a swim in the sun-warmed outdoor pool before getting ready for dinner.

DAY ONE: EVENING

Dinner

Head back to Snug Cove for dinner at **The Beggar's Purse Restaurant** (Orchard Square, Snug Cove; 604–947–0550). This gem is the same place where you had a snack or lunch earlier today, but the bustle has been transformed to a more romantic atmosphere. You may note that some of the artwork has changed, the breakfast signs are gone, the flowers have been replaced, and candles grace the white tablecloths. It's a brilliant way to share expenses for Brad Ovenell-Carter, former restaurant critic for one of BC's major magazines and a veteran restaurateur himself, who has retreated to Bowen for the lifestyle it affords his family. Three or four nights a week, he rustles up a set menu ($28) guaranteed to tempt your palate, with a couple of choices for each course.

For the appetizer you might choose from warm greens with pecan tarragon dressing or spinach, tomato, sweet pepper, and goat cheese terrine with nori. The main course might be a choice of beef tenderloin with chanterelle sauce or sea bass on a fondue of endives with red wine sauce. Then finish off with chocolate mousse or orange crème brûlée. Of course, a tantalizing selection of wines complements whatever you select. The restaurant is open from 6:00 to 8:00 P.M. on Friday, Saturday, and Sunday evenings only; during summer, you may also find it open on Thursday nights. Reservations are highly recommended—make them at the same time as you do your reservations at the Vineyard.

After dinner head back to the Vineyard. On a clear night sit out on the deck on the love seat and watch the last rays of the sun caress the vineyard below you. On cool nights cuddle up in front of the fire or get a video from the main lounge and snuggle up under the puffy quilt. Better still, pull on your suits and have a twenty-minute soak in the hot tub just steps from your room.

Trail Ride with Movie Stars

The sable-colored Norwegian Fjord horses, with a distinctive dark stripe on their manes, are placid and friendly. Two of the Norwegian Fjords joined Evergreen Acres in September 1997, after doing their part in a Disney movie, Eaters of the Dead, filmed in Campbell River on Vancouver Island.

DAY TWO: MORNING

Breakfast

Don't get lazy and sleep through breakfast. It's served in the lounge or in your room by special arrangement. And it's a big one. Depending on the chef's fancy, it could include waffles, eggs Benedict, cheese blintzes, or French toast. Along with all this are heavenly baked goods that you'll be unlikely to get through. Elena will give you a bag, though, and you can take them away with you for an afternoon snack.

Spend your morning saddleback, exploring the island on an ancient breed of horse called the Norwegian Fjord. **Misty Island Trekking at Evergreen Acres,** (1355 Westside Road, Bowen Island; 604–947–2982 or 604–947–2624; from $36 per hour to $72 for half a day) will escort you on an unforgettable tour of the trails and roads of Bowen Island, where you'll meander through the forests and admire views of the ocean. Evergreen Acres has a selection of wonderful Viking cloaks to wrap yourself in when the mist descends, and with your horses from days of old, you'll feel you've stepped back to the twelfth century.

Saddle-weary, head back to the Vineyard to pack up and check out. If you time it right, you'll manage a quick soak in the hot tub to loosen up those muscles before heading out. Savor the last of your breakfast breads on the ferry back to the city—it'll make your time away last just a little bit longer.

FOR MORE ROMANCE

If you're able to squeeze in the time to stay longer and the weather permits doing so, delay your horseback riding until the afternoon and take a sunrise paddle in a kayak. Nothing beats the early-morning stillness before the island wakes. If dragging yourself out of bed in the early morning doesn't appeal, you can go later in the day. **Bowen Island Sea Kayaking** (Box N-56, RR 1, Bowen Island, BC, V0N 1G0; 604–947–9266 or 800–60–KAYAK) can do it all. Or get an early start on your first day and take a walk around **Kilarney Lake** to work up an appetite for lunch. You can walk from Snug Cove on a well-marked trail or drive there (about two minutes). The circle route around the lake is about 4 kilometers round-trip.

ITINERAY 28
Two days and one night

OF STARFISH, BEST FRIENDS, AND SWEET SUMMER CORN: SATURNA ISLAND

*R*emember escaping the house on Saturday morning after you had convinced your parents your chores really were done? Ah, that sense of excitement and anticipation of undiscovered treasures awaiting you. In the tree-dappled sunlight, you cruised the streets on your trusty two-wheeler, rejoicing in the clean fall air and the crunch of fiery fallen leaves.

The day was always perfect when you hooked up with your best friend. You were so close, it seemed the two of you shared the same set of eyes. The same things tickled you or stopped you in wonderment. If there was anyone on earth you wanted to be speechless with, your friend was that person. Remember those days? For you and your love, Saturna Island will be like that.

Saturna has the second largest land area of all the Gulf Islands and yet is the least populated. Many think of it as what the Gulf Islands were like twenty years ago, with a tranquility not often matched. With the second highest mountain in the islands, it seduces you with its stunning views and the driest, sunniest climate in Southwestern British Columbia. You'll leave from Tsawwassen Ferry Terminal for this trip; reservations are a must (see the Appendix).

Practical notes: For tourist information contact **Tourism Vancouver Island** (302–45 Bastion Square, Victoria, BC, V8W 1J1; 250–382–3551; fax 250–382–3523).

DAY ONE: MORNING

For a real weekend away from the hustle and bustle of life, travel to Saturna Island as a foot passenger. Not only will it save you the cost of ferrying your car but it will also put a different slant on your time away. Traveling by ferry is an excursion through sensational Gulf Island waterways. Keep a map at hand to identify the various stops and island villages, or use one of the maps posted on the ferry. A handy camera is essential for wildlife opportunities—dolphins, seals, and whales—and occasional exotic boats or ships. A pensive photo of your love staring at a Chinese junk backlit by the sun will provide memories of this outing for years to come.

The ferry's frequency, duration, and itinerary can vary greatly with the seasons. During the peak summer months, you might be able to travel nonstop between the mainland and the island in an hour; the rest of the year it could take two and a half hours. The milk run through the island is a treat, and the loading and unloading at each stop is a spectator sport among passengers and islanders.

Romance at a Glance

♥ *Rest your head at Saturna Lodge and Restaurant (888–539–8800, 250–539–2254).*

♥ *Cycle the waterfront along Winter Cove Road and East Point Road to the East Point Lighthouse.*

♥ *Enjoy a succulent dinner at Saturna Lodge.*

♥ *Lounge on Saturna Lodge's deck above the minifjord of Boot Cove Bay with a good book, and glide to the hot tub for a change of scene.*

DAY ONE: AFTERNOON

Before you depart on your perfect bike ride, check in at **Saturna Lodge.** The road you drive onto as you exit the ferry, East Point Road, is the main road traversing the island. Follow the road to the first or second right (the two roads, Boot Cove Road

and Payne Road, merge farther up). **Saturna Lodge and Restaurant** (130 Payne Road, Saturna Island; 888–539–8800, $80 to $140, including breakfast) is on your right, immediately after the stop sign.

Styling itself after a French country inn, the lodge has a casual atmosphere and yet is well appointed to appeal to the comfort of its guests. Each of the seven rooms has a wine-related name—Sauterne, Aligote, Tokay, Underugga, Riesling, Napa, Ambrosia. Ask for the Sauterne Suite. It runs the width of the building, with the bathroom at the front of the building and the bed/sitting room at the back. The deck off the bedroom comes equipped with deck chairs to lounge in. The bathroom was made for shared back scrubs—it has a huge double soaker tub you have to climb up into.

Lunch

There really aren't many places to eat on the island, but even if there were, you'd still do well to eat at the lodge. Meals are prepared using fresh organic ingredients and vary daily. Eat on the sundeck outside: It looks out over Boot Cove Bay. Be warned, though, that you don't have to sit too long before island time hits you and you'll have to drag each other away to explore the island. If you prefer, ask the chef to prepare a picnic lunch. Before you head out, be sure to arrange a dining time.

Whether you bike or drive, don't miss **East Point Lighthouse Park,** at the other end of the island. Snowcapped Mount Baker, one of the Pacific Northwest's most dramatic volcanoes, emerges from the mist just across the water from the sculpted sandstone rocks of the park. It's a perfect place for a picnic lunch (or a spectacular vantage point from which to watch sea spume slapped from the waves during storms).

We prefer to use the lodge's complimentary bikes and hitch a ride in the lodge's van past the two eye-popping, thigh-burning hills to the corner of Winter Cove Road and East Point Road. Before setting off to the lighthouse along East Point Road, take a left for a short, 0.5-kilometer cruise to pacific little **Winter Cove Marine Park.** Nestled among small breakwater islands and channels, the cove is a haven for boaters camping their way through the Gulf Islands. In ten minutes or so, you can walk the wide, well-marked trail originating at the east side of the park to some small bluffs overlooking the boat pass to the main channel.

The beach-fringed road to the park is a gentle, 22-kilometer cycle that takes about forty-five to sixty minutes each way. It's nearly all flat, along dramatic views, through stands of shady firs and arbutus. The rocky beaches provide frequent rest stops where you can search for the most unusual natural driftwood sculpture—and gain a kiss for the most creative. Watch for dark floating logs' ends jutting from the water that seem to duck and swim away. Seals are curious animals and will follow you along the beach, rising in the water to get a better look at the unusual island creatures at the edge of their domain.

On some of the rocks, you may see sea lions. Approaching them usually just starts a headlong rush for the open water, but since each weighs more than an ill-tempered ton, don't push your luck. Binoculars are a safe way to observe the social goings-on at the sea-lion shindig. If killer whales are around, pull your camera out and plug your ears. Although orcas are very fond of sea lions, the affection is, alas, unrequited and the ruckus on the ledges can be deafening.

When you're ready to return to the lodge, don't be shy about calling for a ride back over the hills from hell. There is a phone at the park, and the van will meet you at Winter Cove

Park in an hour. A few minutes in the outdoor cedar hot tub will turn your muscles of steel to jelly just in time for a glass of wine. Big furry robes are supplied.

DAY ONE: EVENING
Dinner

Dinner at the lodge, at the outer edge of Canada, is a meal worthy of any first-class restaurant, at about one-third the price. Each night is a different prix fixe, three-course dinner for $20. You might choose from fresh coho salmon steamed with red chili broth and saffron rice or peppered rib-eye steak with mushroom spaetzle, followed by chocolate mousse trifle or poached pears in red wine sauce and fennel pepper cream. The setting is intimate and romantic, with low candles and the setting sun lending a glow to the room.

By spring of the year 2000, the first bottles from the lodge's own vineyards will be available. Until then, connoisseurs or just friends of the grape can take advantage of the considerable knowledge of the lodge's cohosts, and appreciative aficionados may be able to pry a little of the lodge's secret stash from its hiding place.

The wine industry in British Columbia has attracted some high-caliber talent from the vineyards of Europe, eager to try out new ideas away from the tradition-bound wine culture of the Continent. The dry climate of the interior and a few microclimates of the Southwest Coast are beginning to produce some rich, world-class vintages. A trip to the vineyards a few kilometers away under the cliffs of Mount Warburton Pike and the nearby beaches is worthwhile after your hike tomorrow.

Following the tradition of the isolated miners and loggers of the coast in days gone by, on many nights the hosts and guests have an impromptu music session after dinner. Spoons can be provided for the musically challenged, and no voices are spurned.

DAY TWO: MORNING

Breakfast

In the dining room choose the seat nearest the picture window overlooking the cove. Linger over the organic breakfast, served with coffee imported by float plane from the Italian district of Vancouver. Peruse the art books and coastal histories from the library. You can fritter away most of the morning in unhurried reading.

❧

After breakfast drive or ask for a lift to the top of **Mount Warburton Pike** for a stunning panorama of the surrounding islands, the snowcapped Olympic Range in Washington State, Victoria, and the Strait of Georgia. Dress warmly in all but the sunniest weather. There are almost always spectacular aerial displays by ravens, hawks, and the occasional eagle riding the thermals. On some days it's so still that you can hear the ravens' wings beat as they cavort through the sunshine. For a couple in love, this is a truly magical place.

The walk back to the lodge takes no more than an hour, all downhill, through mountain forest. Before your sojourn to the top, do ask for a late checkout: The pure sea air, a little reading, and a soft shoulder have been known to suggest the need for a wee nap.

FOR MORE ROMANCE

Nothing brings home that edge-of-the-world feeling as fast as transferring directly from a 747 at the airport or your downtown luxury hotel to a seaplane. The view out over the islands and the landing is a kick. **Harbour Air** (in Vancouver call 604–688–1277 or, outside Vancouver, 800–665–0212) has scheduled seaplane flights from downtown Vancouver Harbour, Victoria Harbour, and the Vancouver Airport Seaplane Harbour.

ITINERARY 29
Two days and two nights

TWO ISLANDS MAKING A PASS:
GALIANO AND MAYNE ISLANDS

*S*tep into rural England on Galiano Island. It starts with the lambs that greet you as you turn up the drive to the Bellhouse Inn. The print-fabric, overstuffed chairs and chesterfield in the lounge positioned to survey the lawns and water add to the effect. As you'd expect in any good English inn, tea and coffee are delivered on a tray outside your door in the morning, and a decanter of sherry graces the bureau for those who relish a tipple before bed. Would you guess that both owners hail from England?

Practical notes: Contact the **Galiano Island Chamber of Commerce Travel Infocentre** (P.O Box 73, Galiano Island, BC, V0N 1P0; phone/fax 250–539–2233) for information on the island, and have a look at the Appendix. (*Note:* A minimum stay of two nights is required at the Bellhouse Inn for July and August weekends. This itinerary can be tailored to one night by simply dropping the Mayne Island exploration lunch and walk.)

DAY ONE: MORNING

While the **Gulf Islands** have much to offer at any time of the year, our favorite season starts right after Labor Day, when the weather is still warm, many of the businesses are still open, but the crowds have thinned. To get to Galiano Island, go to the Tsawwassen Ferry Terminal to catch the ferry to **Sturdies Bay.** If you haven't already eaten, you can get a full breakfast or a Danish and tea or coffee onboard and then meander the decks to admire the vistas of the mountains of the mainland and the panorama of the **Strait of Georgia.** Sturdies Bay is the first ferry stop just out of the open waters of the Strait of Georgia and into **Active Pass,** a major shipping and boating passage between the inner Gulf Islands and the strait. Caught between high bluffs and wiggling through a curvy passage between **Mayne** and **Galiano Islands,** the water route here is narrow and the fast-flowing current treacherous. As you approach Active Pass, the old red-and-white-fashion lighthouse on your left is on Mayne Island, which you will visit this trip. During the voyage keep your eyes peeled for whales.

Drive off the ferry onto Sturdies Bay Road. Turn left onto Burril Road; turn left again at Jack Road and then right onto Farmhouse Road. The Bellhouse Inn is the first lane on your left, just past the grazing sheep. (If you decide to go carless, talk to your hosts and they'll pick you up at the ferry, probably in the Bellhouse's vintage car, a 1935 Bentley.) **The Bellhouse Inn** (29 Farmhouse Road, Galiano Island; 800–970–RING [7464] or 250–539–5667; fax: 250–539–5316; $89 to $125, including breakfast) is a delight. It was built as a farmhouse in the 1890s but became an inn in 1920. The owners, Andrea Porter and David Birchall, made sure none of the charm and character of the house was lost when they renovated in 1995. All the rooms now have private balconies and private bathrooms and are decorated

Romance at a Glance

♥ *Stay at the Bellhouse Inn for the comfort of an intimate English country inn (800–970–RING [7464] or 250–539–5667).*

♥ *Kayak around the island with Galiano Island Sea Kayaking (250–539–5390).*

♥ *Chow down at the Hummingbird Pub (250–539–5472).*

♥ *Visit Mayne Island for an afternoon.*

♥ *Lunch and lounge on the veranda of the Springwater Lodge (250–539–5521).*

to suit the building's history. One of the most marvelous features of the inn is its location on the waters of Active Pass.

The Bellhouse Inn has only four rooms in the main house, so it's essential that you call ahead to reserve. When you do, ask for the Kingfisher Room. Its color scheme of rich cream and soft greens, with accents of muted rose, creates an enchanting room. The double French doors open to the deck looking out over the waters of Active Pass and catching the warm southern sun.

DAY ONE: AFTERNOON
Lunch

After checking in at the Bellhouse, hop back in your car and head to **Montague Harbour Marina** (250–539–5733) for lunch. Go back to Sturdies Bay Road and turn left (away from the ferry terminal) until you reach Montague Park Road; turn left again, and drive to nearly the end of the road. (The marina is just before the actual end of the road at the campground.) Park your car and head down to the waterfront to the restaurant for a bite to eat. The cheerful blue and white building, with window boxes stuffed with masses of red and pink pansies and impatiens, complement the bustle of colorful sails and small pleasure-boats that call at the bay. Sit out on the sun-drenched deck under the blue and white umbrellas and have a light lunch. The eclectic menu features a good Greek hummus and tzatziki, as well as an organic carrot cake guaranteed to give you a sugar buzz.

❧

After lunch call the nearby **Galiano Island Sea Kayaking** (637 Southwind Road, Galiano Island, BC, V0N 1P0; phone/fax: 250–539–5390; $19 per person for a two-hour guided tour, with a lesson, or a four-hour rental; longer tours available) for your afternoon excursion on the sheltered waters around the bay. It's better to reserve your adventure before lunch but the outfit does accommodate last-minute trips so you can go as the mood suits you. The firm's base is nearby in the harbor, so you can call for directions or staff will fetch you.

When you call to reserve, ask for a double kayak so that you can share the experience without having to shout across the water. Even if you have never kayaked before, don't be shy. You don't need experience. The friendly people at Galiano Island Sea Kayaking will include an introductory lesson in your tour. Staff will equip you with a waterproof suit, a lifejacket, and everything you need to enjoy your afternoon.

DAY ONE: EVENING
Dinner

Go casual and head to the **Hummingbird Pub** (47 Sturdies Bay Road; 250–539–5472, $7 to $12) for dinner. The atmosphere is a mix of English pub and rural diner, with typical pub food of burgers, salads, fish-and-chips, and the like. If it's really warm, you can sit outside on the deck among the trees and enjoy the evening. After eating, try your hand at one of the pool tables before heading back to peruse the library in the Bellhouse's guest lounge.

DAY TWO: MORNING

Breakfast

If the weather is warm enough, throw open the doors to watch the activity as you lie in bed and drink your tea. Relish your cozy twosome and have your breakfast in the room. Idling in the wicker chairs placed in front of the French doors, watching the passing parade of pleasurecraft and small ships, is a grand way to enjoy your breakfast if you don't want to go downstairs to join the other guests. Do try the Bellhouse Benedict, with salmon and homemade muffins, a lovely taste treat. To extend the lazy morning, try the view from the double hammock, or swim at the sandy beach in front of the house. The lambs also accept any gifts of pears or apples picked from the trees on the property.

ﮦﻬ

When you grow more energetic, take a drive over to **Bluffs Park** for a top-down view of Active Pass and the channel beyond. Bluffs Park was purchased by a group of islanders many years ago for everyone to enjoy, and the owner donated another huge plot to supplement the islanders' purchase. There are two ways to get to Bluffs Park. The easiest and shortest is to turn right onto Farmhouse Road from the Bellhouse, turn left onto Jack Road, and left onto Burrill Road, which shortly becomes Bluff Road. Continue to the PARK ENTRANCE sign and take the first left to drive to the view. All of these are short distances. The road extends out the other side of the park and will eventually bring you back to the ferry, but it's far steeper and bumpier.

DAY TWO: AFTERNOON

For the afternoon take the ferry across Active Pass to explore Mayne Island. On most days the ferry to Mayne will depart Galiano sometime in the late morning and return in the late afternoon or early evening. For the $8.00 fare it's a cheap way to sightsee the whole Active Pass area and take in Mayne Island. When you land on Mayne, take a left from the ferry onto Village Bay Road (a block away), turn right, and travel to the village center. When you come to the T junction in the village, turn toward the water, past the red government docks and the Springwater Lodge along Georgina Point Road. At the very end of Georgina Point Road is the **Active Pass Lighthouse** (open daily from 1:00 to 3:00 P.M.). Built in 1885, the picturesque red-and-white structure has undergone several rebuilds and renovations but still retains yesterday's charm. There is a spectacular panorama of the Coast Range on the mainland, and the rock formations of the foreshore are worth a gander and a stroll. If you enter the small meadow to the right of the lighthouse on tiptoes, you might be able to glimpse deer that frequent the area.

For an appetite builder and a stunning view of the other side of the island, pass back across half the island to the Springwater Lodge and the government docks. Instead of turning right, back toward the ferry, continue on through the village on Fernhill Road, past the fire hall and school to Montrose Road, on the right. At the corner is **Mayne Open Market** (also known as MOM's; 250–539–5024), where you can pick up snacks and refreshments for your walk. A block behind MOM's is the parking lot for the well-marked walk up to the ridge. The trail is in good condition, and a forty-five-minute walk brings you to the top, where you can meander arm-in-arm for another forty-five minutes along the ridge line. You'll find several promontories and lookouts here, and you may have to stop to whisper promises or secrets to one another.

Lunch

If you're feeling less energetic, skip the walk and plant yourself on the sunny deck of the **Springwater Lodge** (at Miner's Bay; 250–539–5521; open year-round; $6 to $12 for lunch), in front of the government docks in the village. The food is typical pub fare but pleasing, and the view of Active Pass is unrivaled. On most days you'll find a seal or two looking longingly at your fish-and-chips from the waters around the dock.

❦

Whether you decide to return to the Bellhouse for another night or return to Vancouver from Mayne, be sure to check the ferry schedules closely. A missed ferry could lead to an exciting adventure. . . or it might not.

FOR MORE ROMANCE

As a lazier alternative for your first afternoon on Galiano, you can join others for a catamaran sail among the islands aboard the 46-foot catamaran ***Great White Cloud*** (637 Southwind Road, Galiano Island, BC, V0N 1P0; phone/fax: 250–539–5390; rates start at $39 per person). For the animal enthusiast there are summer excursions to **Ballengall Nature Park** on Salt Spring Island that are sometimes accompanied by a naturalist. Other voyages are for secluded beach picnics at "one of the loveliest white sand beaches in the islands," according to boat-captain Tom Hennessy. Passengers are treated to a lunch of smoked salmon, fruit salad, white wine, and dessert, and can beachcomb or swim from the boat or shore. The four-hour trip rewards you with a little taste of the smaller islands you cannot see by ferry.

BC FERRIES

BC Ferries is the most convenient and economical way to access the places mentioned in the Vancouver Island and Ferry Tales Itineraries.

The city of Vancouver, British Columbia, is on the mainland, a ninety-minute ferry ride from Victoria, the capital of the province. The Gulf Islands are scattered in the waters between Vancouver on the mainland and Vancouver Island. Traveling time to the islands depends greatly on the island involved, the time of year, and the time of week that you travel.

PRICES

The price for the ferry from Vancouver to Vancouver Island is approximately $23 to $32 for the car; the price for each passenger is $7.50 to $9.00. Both rates depend on the time of year and the day of the week you travel. Individual rates to the Gulf Islands vary greatly and need to be checked with BC Ferries directly.

THE TERMINALS

There are two major ferry terminals in the Lower Mainland to which we direct you. One is not far from the U.S. border and is called the Tsawwassen Terminal. This ferry will take you into Swartz Bay Ferry Terminal on Vancouver Island and to the Gulf Islands of Galiano, Saturna, and Salt Spring; Swartz Bay Ferry Terminal is the arrival point for traveling to Victoria, Sooke, and the Malahat.

To get to the Tsawwassen Terminal, take Highway 99 south to Highway 17.

The other ferry terminal is the Horse-shoe Bay Terminal, which is used to go to Bowen Island and to the Departure Bay Ferry Terminal in Nanaimo, in the middle of Vancouver Island, for easy access to Tofino on the West Coast of Vancouver Island. To get to the Horseshoe Bay Ferry Terminal, take Highway 1 west.

Note: A new ferry terminal, Duke Point, lies just south of Nanaimo, and is used to cross between Nanaimo and the Tsawwassen Ferry Terminal. This option might be more convenient when you are going to the West Coast of Vancouver Island, depending on your starting point on the mainland.

PRACTICAL FERRY NOTES

• Arrive at the terminal in plenty of time—generally, forty-five minutes prior to departure during nonbusy periods. During the peak season it's important to get there even earlier. When departing some of the Gulf Islands, arriving twenty minutes prior to departure will suffice.

• Always phone to confirm ferry times. Summertime, holidays, and weather can create extensive changes in the schedule.
On some ferry routes you must have a reservation to travel. Don't get caught without one.

• Food and passenger services vary by vessel. Each of the ferries has a cafeteria, a snack bar, a gift shop, and a newsstand onboard. Depending on the ship, you will also find more extensive dining options.

CONTACT NUMBERS

BC Ferries: (888) 223-3779 or (250) 386-3431.

ANNUAL EVENTS

Following are some of the special events that take place around Vancouver. When you're planning your trip, call **Tourism Vancouver** (604–683–2000) for specific dates or give a call directly to the number listed. Tourism Vancouver can also tell you about such things as museum exhibits, plays, and sporting events.

For similar information on Victoria, call **Tourism Victoria** (250–953–2033). For any of the Gulf Islands, call the number recommended at the beginning of the itinerary on that island.

JANUARY

Polar Bear Swim. The hardy take a plunge into the Pacific Ocean at English Bay Beach on the first day of January.

Chinese New Year. Late January or early February. Celebrations and events at the Chinese Cultural Centre (604–687–0729) and the Dr. Sun Yat-Sen Classical Chinese Garden (604–662–3207).

MARCH

Vancouver Playhouse International Wine Festival. Late March/early April, for seven days. (604)–873–3311.

Whale-Watching Season on Vancouver Island. (250) 725–3414.

Whale Festival. Middle to late March. (250) 725–3414.

APRIL

Terrific Jazz Party. Late April, at different venues throughout Victoria. (250) 953–2011.

MAY

Vancouver International Marathon. (604) 872–2928.

Cloverdale Rodeo. Three days in mid-May. (604) 576–9461.

JUNE

International Jazz Festival. Ten days in June. (604) 682–0706.

Bard on the Beach. June through September. Theater on the beach. (604) 739–0559.

Canadian International Dragon Boat Festival. Three days in June. (604) 688–2382.

JULY

Symphony of Fire. End of July/early August. Fireworks competition. (604) 738–4304.

Vancouver International Comedy Festival. End of July/early August. (604) 683–0883.

Vancouver Folk Music Festival. Latter part of July and events throughout the year. (604) 602–9798.

Canada Day. July 1. Nonstop live entertainment at Canada Place. (604) 666–8477.

Steveston Salmon Festival. July 1. (604) 277–6812.

Roots Weekend. In Whistler. (604) 932–2394.

AUGUST

BC Day. First Monday in August.

Abbottsford AirShow. Second weekend in August. (604) 852–8511.

Indy Vancouver Car Race. Labour Day Weekend. (604) 280–INDY.

Pacific National Exhibition. Late August to early September.

(604) 253–2311.

SEPTEMBER

Vancouver International Fringe Festival. Mid September. (604) 257–0350.

Terry Fox Run. Second Sunday after Labour Day. (604) 464–2666 or (800) 665–8369.

Whistler Jazz and Blues Festival. Late September. (604) 932–2394.

Whistler's Really Big Street Fest. Early September. (604) 932–2394.

NOVEMBER

Circle Craft Christmas Market. Takes place the weekend closest to Remembrance Day, November 11. (604) 801–5220.

DECEMBER

Boxing Day. December 26.

Carol Ships, Parade of Lights. Throughout December. (604) 878–9988.

Festival of Lights at VanDusen Botanical Garden. Mid-December to early January. (604) 878–9274.

Christmas at Canada Place. Early December to early January. (604) 666–8477.

GENERAL INDEX

Note: For Restaurant, Hotel, and Nightlife listings, see the special indexes, which begin on page 241.

ROMANTIC RESTAURANTS

Restaurant price categories in this index, represented by one to three dollar signs, designate the cost of an entree for one person. Each category is indicated in the following key IN CANADIAN DOLLARS

Inexpensive ($): Under $10   Moderate ($$): $10 to $20   Expensive ($$$): More than $20

Asian
Chao Phraya Thai Restaurant ($-$$),
  1505 West 2 Avenue, 11
Floata Seafood Restaurant ($-$$),
  400-180 Keefer Street, 102
Phnom Penh Restaurant ($-$$),
  244 E Georgia Street, 105
Seacourt Restaurant ($$-$$$),
  149 Fulford Ganges Road,
  Salt Spring Island, 206

Brunch
Boathouse, The ($-$$),
  Westminster Quay, New Westminster, 77
Bacchus Restaurant ($$),
  Wedgewood Hotel, 63
Cafe Pacifica ($),
  300-999 Canada Place, 123

Remington's Restaurant ($-$$),
  Plaza 500 Hotel, 32
Kipling's ($$),
  The Empress, Victoria, 171
Milestones ($),
  1210 Denman Street, 68
Milestones Inner Harbour ($),
  812 Wharf Street, Victoria, 171
Riley Cafe, The ($-$$),
  1661 Granville Street, 4

Breakfast
Auntie Em's Kitchen ($),
  129-4340 Lorimer Road, Whistler, 148
Breakfast Cafe, The ($),
  Orchard Square, Snug Cove, 212
Crepe Montagne ($),
  116-4368 Main Street, Whistler, 148

ROMANTIC PLACES TO STAY

NIGHTLIFE